A PRACTICAL GUIDE
TO THE EVALUATION OF
SEXUAL ABUSE
IN THE PREPUBERTAL CHILD

This manual is dedicated to the staff at the
Children's Hospital of Philadelphia and the Center for
Children's Support at the University of Medicine
and Dentistry of New Jersey,
who work to provide the best possible care
to children suspected of being sexually abused.

A PRACTICAL GUIDE
TO THE EVALUATION OF
SEXUAL ABUSE
IN THE PREPUBERTAL CHILD

Angelo P. Giardino, MD, MSEd
Martin A. Finkel, DO, FACOP
Eileen R. Giardino, PhD, RN, MSN
Toni Seidl, MSW, ACSW
Stephen Ludwig, MD, FAAP

SAGE PUBLICATIONS
International Educational and Professional Publisher
Newbury Park London New Delhi

For information address:

SAGE Publications, Inc.
2455 Teller Road
Newbury Park, California 91320

SAGE Publications Ltd.
6 Bonhill Street
London EC2A 4PU
United Kingdom

SAGE Publications India Pvt. Ltd.
M-32 Market
Greater Kailash I
New Delhi 110 048 India

Printed in the United States of America

Library of Congress Cataloging-in-Publication Data

Main entry under title:

A Practical guide to the evaluation of sexual abuse in the prepubertal child / Angelo P. Giardino . . . [et al.]; with contributions by Julie Lippman, Esther Deblinger-Sosland.
  p.   cm.
  Includes bibliographical references and index.
  ISBN 0-8039-4815-8 (cloth)
    1. Sexually abused children—Identification. 2. Sexually abused children—Medical exwamiations. I. Giardino, Angelo P.
RJ507.S49P7 1992
618.92′65—dc20   92-27864

92 93 94 95 10 9 8 7 6 5 4 3 2 1

Sage Production Editor: Diane S. Foster

Contents

Foreword
  Suzanne M. Sgroi   ix

Preface   xiii

Acknowledgments   xv

1. **The Problem**   1
   Definition   2
   Scope of the Problem: Incidence and Prevalence   2
   Categories Included in Sexual Abuse   5
   Conceptual Models   6
   Preconditions for Sexual Abuse   7
     Motivation of the Perpetrator   7
     Overcoming Internal Inhibitions   7
     Overcoming External Inhibitions   7
     Overcoming a Child's Resistance   7
   Characteristics of the Perpetrator   8
   Individuality of the Nature of Sexual Abuse   8
   Longitudinal Progression of Sexual Abuse   8
     Engagement   9
     Sexual Interaction   9
     Secrecy   9
     Disclosure   9
     Suppression   9
   Child Sexual Abuse Accommodation Syndrome   10
   Long-Term Effects of Sexual Abuse   10

Issues of Power and Control   11
In Brief   11

2. **The Evaluation**   **13**
Approach to Evaluation of Sexual Abuse   15
Emergent Evaluation   15
History   16
Physical Examination   17
Laboratory Studies   18
Documentation   18
In Brief   18

3. **Interview and History**   **19**
Interview as Diagnostic and Therapeutic   20
The Interview Process   22
     Phase 1: Warm-Up   22
     Phase 2: Caregiver Interview   23
     Phase 3: Child Interview   23
         Developmental/Cognitive/Language Issues   24
         Types of Questions: Open-Ended to
         Closed-Ended Continuum   25
     Wrap-Up Session   25
Compliance With Legal Responsibilities   28
In Brief   28

4. **Physical Examination and Laboratory Specimens**   **29**
Physical Examination   29
Familiarity With the Prepubertal Examination   30
Laboratory Findings   30
Lack of Evidence   30
PREPUBERTAL ANATOMY   **31**
Basic Anatomy and Development   31
     Diagrams of Normal Anatomy   32
Estrogen Effect on Female Genitalia: Huffman Stages   36
Outward Sexual Development: Tanner Stages   36
     Pubic Hair: Male and Female   36
     Breast Development   40
     Male Genitalia   42
Normal Female Genitalia   42
     Mons Pubis   42
     Labia Majora   42
     Labia Minora   42
     Clitoris   43
     Urethral Meatus   43
     Vaginal Vestibule   43
     Hymen   43
     Fossa Navicularis   44
     Posterior Fourchette   44
     Normal Variants of Hymenal Anatomy   45
Male Anatomy   49
     Penis   49
     Scrotum   49

Testis   49
Epididymis   50
Anal Anatomy   50
FINDINGS IN SEXUAL ABUSE   51
Variables Affecting Physical Evidence   51
Findings in Sexual Abuse   51
Degree of Physical Contact   52
Extragenital Trauma   52
Fondling and Digital Penetration   53
Male Abusive Findings   55
Anal Examination Findings   55
Penile Contact With Genitalia and Anus   57
Oral-Genital Contact   59
Penile Penetration   59
Summary of Abuse Findings   62
Hymenal Orifice   64
Anal Penetration   64
Accidental Trauma   65
THE PHYSICAL EXAMINATION   66
Preparing for the Physical Examination of the Child   66
Tools of the Physical Examination   67
Method of Evaluation   67
Genital and Perianal Examination   68
Lighting and Privacy   68
Positioning   69
Examining the External and Internal Structures   71
Vaginal Vestibule   72
Size of Hymenal Orifice   72
Anus and Perianal Area   73
LABORATORY EVALUATION   75
Collection of Specimens   75
Standard Studies   76
Forensic Evidence   77
Documenting Sexual Contact and Identifying
the Perpetrator (De Jong, 1988)   78
Description   78
Collection of Specimens   79
In Brief   80

5. Differential Diagnosis of Anogenital Findings   82
Framework for Consideration   83
Categorization and Etiologic Differential Diagnosis   83
Anogenital Erythema, Excoriation, Pruritus   84
Local Irritation   85
Dermatologic   85
Infections   86
Systemic   88
Anogenital Bruising   89
Local Injury   89
Dermatologic   90
Systemic   91
Anogenital Bleeding and/or Bloody Vaginal Discharge   92

Local Irritation   92
Dermatologic   92
Infection   92
Endocrinologic   92
Structural/Neoplastic   93
Nonbloody Vaginal Discharge   94
Unusual Anatomic Appearance   95
Acquired   95
Congenital   97

6. Sexually Transmitted Diseases   100
Gonorrhea   101
Chlamydia Trachomatis   103
Syphilis   104
Condyloma Acuminata   106
Trichomoniasis   107
Herpes Genitalis   108
HIV   109
Pediculosis Pubis   110
Gardnerella Vaginalis   110
Chancroid and Granuloma Inguinale   111
Candida   112
In Brief   112

7. Mental Health Evaluation   113
Julie Lippmann and Esther Deblinger
Referrals   114
Purpose of the Mental Health Evaluation   115
Interviewing the Child   115
Aspects of Validation   117
Assessment of Emotional Impact   118
Post-Traumatic Stress Disorder   119
Inappropriate Sexual Behaviors   120
Interviewing Other Family Members   121
Feedback and Recommendations for Treatment   124
Prognosis   125
Treatment   126

8. Documentation and Conclusions   128
Detail of the Medical Record   128
Recording the History   128
Recording the Physical Examination   130
Court Testimony   131
Conclusion   133
In Brief   135
Do's   135
Don'ts   135

References   136

Index   143

About the Authors   149

Foreword

My first encounter with a child victim of sexual abuse occurred in 1972, when I was working part-time in a VD clinic run by a city health department. The child was 6 years old and he had been brought to the clinic by his mother. She handed me two documents. One was a note written on a prescription form by a pediatrician they had consulted the previous day. He had told her to bring the boy to the VD clinic and give the note to the staff. The note read, "Suspect gonorrhea, please treat!" The other document was a carbon copy of an emergency room record. It reflected that the boy had been treated one month earlier in the emergency room (with an adequate dose of penicillin) for gonococcal urethritis. The instructions to the mother included admonition to "Watch your child!" and "Scrub your toilet seat!"

The boy looked embarrassed and frightened; his mother was grim and defiant. "He's got it again," she said. "He didn't get it from my toilet seat. I scrub it with Lysol every day! Where is he getting this from?" she demanded. Where indeed? And what to do about it? A glance at the creamy white discharge emanating from the child's urethral meatus and staining his underwear convinced me that the pediatrician and the emergency room physician both had diagnosed the infection accurately. The boy had acute recurrent gonococcal urethritis (later confirmed by smears and cultures). It was obvious that his infection was not resulting from contact with a toilet seat. I was certain that the child had been sexually victimized by someone who had a gonococcal infection. Beyond the neonatal period, gonorrhea is transmitted by sexual contact, not by contact with toilet seats! However, convincing others that the boy had been sexually abused did not prove to be an easy matter.

No one in the clinic was willing to view the boy as a victim of child abuse. An older and more experienced staff physician suggested that the sociocultural influences of growing up in a poor family had caused the youngster to become promiscuous at an early age. Undoubtedly, my colleague suggested, our 6-year-old patient had acquired these infections from consenting sexual activity with an equally promiscuous age-mate. Rational opposition to this hypothesis seemed pointless at the time. I was too preoccupied by my own inability to elicit information from the child or his mother about what really had occurred. Naturally, I went about it in the wrong way, communicating much of my anxiety and frustration to them. Also, I made the common error of questioning them in each other's presence instead of interviewing them separately.

Treating the infection was easy; identifying the underlying causes and facilitating child protection were not. The clinic staff were horrified to learn that I proposed to report the case to child protective services immediately. They were worried about violating the public health code, which, at that time, ensured confidentiality of VD reports but did not speak to the relationship between sexually transmitted diseases in children and sexual abuse. When I called child protective services anyway to report the case, I was told that the agency was overwhelmed by complaints of physical abuse of children and that the staff had received no instructions about investigating complaints of child sexual abuse, probably because they rarely received such complaints. Furthermore, I was told that the statutory child protection agency had never received a complaint of sexual abuse for a diagnosis of gonorrhea in a child and that it was unlikely that this complaint would be pursued, since the city health department was "taking care of it."

What a mess! Eventually, a savvy public health nurse unraveled the mystery, at least to a point. She followed the existing protocol for contact investigation of gonorrhea infections in persons 10 years of age or under. This involved obtaining cultures from all household contacts of the infected child, whether or not they were symptomatic. In this way, asymptomatic infections in a 4-year-old sister and a 14-year-old uncle of my patient were discovered. In a private interview, the little girl confided to the nurse that the adolescent uncle sometimes "played games" with his niece and nephew while he was baby-sitting for them. First, the older boy would masturbate himself; then he would fondle and masturbate the younger children with hands contaminated with his own genital secretions. The games included the uncle's coercing the little boy and girl to mimic his behavior and masturbate him as well as to perform oral sex on him. The younger children did not enjoy the games, but cooperated because they were afraid of retaliation by the older boy if they told on him.

Case solved, right? Not really. From whom did the uncle learn this behavior? What more was needed to protect all of the minors living in this home from repeated intergenerational sexual contact? What indeed?

Whenever I relate this story, I remember by own frustration about the total lack of guidelines available in 1972 for responsible intervention in cases of child sexual abuse. I should know—I looked hard and carefully, first at the medical literature and then in the broader field of behavioral sciences. Only one reference (Branch & Paxton, 1965) addressed realistically the relationship between childhood gonorrhea and a history of sexual contact. A widely quoted reference (Shore & Winkelstein, 1971) describing nonsexual transmission of gonorrhea to Eskimo children was based on inaccurate information due to the authors' unfamiliarity with the language and culture of the subjects who were studied (Thompson, 1988). When I performed a comprehensive literature search for my first article on child sexual abuse (Sgroi, 1975), I could find no references on medical evaluation of children for sexual abuse. Nothing was available to assist health professionals to perform careful and comprehensive examinations. No one had yet published articles or chapters or books that addressed the critical interface among medicine, child protective services, law enforcement, and the behavioral sciences that is so necessary for appropriate intervention.

I have shared this personal historical perspective to celebrate a significant change for the better. There is now a proliferation of helpful and enlightening publications about child sexual abuse intervention. This manual will help health professionals, especially physicians, nurse practitioners, and physicians' assistants, to find their way through a sometimes bewildering array of data and references. The manual provides up-to-date protocols and guidelines for all aspects of medical evaluation of sexual abuse in prepubertal children. The authors are to be congratulated for their contribution to the field. How I wish that I had been able to find a comparable guide to manage my first case!

SUZANNE M. SGROI, M.D.
Executive Director, New England Clinical Associates
West Hartford, Connecticut

Preface

The purpose of this manual is to serve as a reference guide for health care professionals called upon to evaluate children suspected of having been sexually abused. The intended audience spans a number of professions, and is not limited to physicians and nurses. Therefore, we envision this manual as a helpful tool for various members of the health care team, including clinical social workers, psychologists/psychiatrists, child protective service workers, and law enforcement personnel. Because there are diverse primary care providers who evaluate children in a variety of settings, we use the inclusive term *health care professionals* rather than more specific professional titles to refer to the health care providers involved in the evaluation. This manual provides the health care professional with background information on the topic of sexual abuse. This information then serves as a foundation upon which the evaluator can build an orderly procedure for the evaluation of the child. The manual is not intended to be a compendium of all that is known or proposed concerning sexual victimization; rather, it serves as

---

AUTHORS' NOTE: Every effort has been made to ensure that drug dosages and recommended usages given in this manual are accurate and conform to accepted standards at the time of publication. However, the reader is advised to consult printed information on each drug and its use prior to administering any medication, especially when using infrequently used drugs.

a reference guide for the identification, evaluation, and documentation of suspected sexual abuse.

We believe that use of this manual will increase the awareness of health care professionals concerning sexual abuse. The manual will (a) increase the consideration of sexual abuse in the differential diagnosis given specific and nonspecific signs and symptoms, (b) reassure health care professionals in their role as health care providers and child advocates, and (c) provide a reference on how to proceed with the medical and psychological assessment, with emphasis on the history, physical and genital examination, pertinent laboratory studies, and documentation.

Because health care professionals play a primary role in the medical evaluation of abuse victims, they need to utilize a comprehensive approach in the evaluation of suspected sexual abuse cases. The medical evaluation should occur in the context of a multidisciplinary team approach to the child. It should include a history, laboratory studies, and a physical assessment that includes a thorough examination of the genital area. In all cases of suspected abuse, it is essential that the specific findings of all interviews and examinations be carefully documented.

The underlying goal of this manual is to enable examining health care professionals to become more knowledgeable and comfortable with the evaluation of children suspected of having been sexually abused. As examiners become more comfortable with the evaluation of child sexual abuse, they will be better able to generate a supportive and comfortable environment for children, and for those children's caregivers as well.

ANGELO P. GIARDINO
MARTIN A. FINKEL
EILEEN R. GIARDINO
TONI SEIDL
STEPHEN LUDWIG

Acknowledgments

We would like to thank the following for their assistance in the production of the manual and their willingness to share their materials:

Cindy W. Christian, M.D.
Allan R. De Jong, M.D.
John W. Duckett, M.D.
Marcia Herman-Giddens, P.A., M.P.H.
David A. Horowitz, M.D.
Charles F. Johnson, M.D.
Suzy Kravitz Miller, M.D.
Gail Slap, M.D.
Howard M. Snyder, M.D.
Alan Woolf, M.D., M.P.H.

The Advisor, American Professional Society on the Abuse of Children
Journal of Adolescent Health Care
Morbidity and Mortality Weekly, Centers for Disease Control
Patient Care
Pediatrics
Pediatrics in Review

Williams and Wilkins Company
Wolters-Noordhoff

Margi Ide, Photography (Medical Education Center, Children's Hospital of Philadelphia, PA)

Karen Ott and Christine Jones, Illustration Services (Biomedical Communications, University of Pennsylvania, Philadelphia)

Larry Stein, Medical Illustrator (Medigraphics, Mt. Holly, NJ)

Nursing Staff of the Emergency Department, Children's Hospital of Philadelphia

Pediatric Housestaff, Children's Hospital of Philadelphia

Beryl Miller, Administrative Assistant, Robert Wood Johnson Clinical Scholar's Program, University of Pennsylvania School of Medicine, Philadelphia

1 The Problem

The number of reported cases of sexual abuse of children has dramatically increased in the last 10 years (Krugman, 1986). Reasons proposed for the rise in the number of reported cases include (a) an increased openness in society for the discussion of sexually related topics; (b) an increased awareness of the problem of sexual abuse on the part of both the general public and child health care professionals; and (c) a greater awareness of abusive behavior patterns as well as identification of children at risk for victimization. Despite greater awareness, the majority of cases of sexual abuse still go unreported. It has been estimated that only one-fourth to one-third of all incidents of child abuse are known to child-care professionals (Finkelhor & Hotaling, 1983; Herman-Giddens & Frothingham, 1987).

Historically, the reasons for failure on the part of health care professionals to recognize the signs and symptoms of sexual abuse of children have included the following: social and cultural taboos, personal values, anxiety surrounding discussion of the topic, denial, and relative lack of medical knowledge about the victimization of children and its presentation (Herman-Giddens & Frothingham, 1987; Horowitz, 1987; Ladson, Johnson, & Doty, 1987). These barriers are beginning to disappear as health care professionals become more knowledgeable about the victimization of children and thus more readily able to acknowledge the existence of the problem and to intervene in a timely fashion. Sgroi (1975) states that a prerequisite for the diagnosis of sexual abuse is the willingness of the health care professional to consider the possibility that abuse may occur.

Definition

Sexual abuse is a complex medical and social problem, with literature reflecting the varied nature of child victimization through diverse definitions. In this manual, we utilize a composite definition of sexual abuse, combining the definitions of Kempe (1978) and Sgroi (1982). As used here, the term *sexual abuse* refers to the involvement in sexual activities by an older person of a dependent, developmentally immature child or adolescent for that older person's own sexual stimulation, or for the gratification of other persons, as in child pornography or prostitution. Abusive activities include exhibitionism, sexualized kissing, fondling, masturbation, digital or object penetration of the vagina or anus, and oral-genital, genital-genital, and anal-genital contact (Faller, 1988; Kempe, 1978; Seidl & Paradise, 1984; Sgroi, 1982). The sexual act is imposed on a child or an adolescent who cannot provide informed consent because of his or her age or developmental stage (Kempe, 1978). Central to the concept of sexual abuse are the misuse of power and the betrayal of a child's trust by an older individual (Seidl & Paradise, 1984).

The essential components of the definition of sexual abuse involve the child's developmental immaturity and inability to consent, and the perpetrator's abuse of power and relationship. In sexual abuse, the perpetrator has authority and power over the child ascribed by his or her age, and is thus able, implicitly or directly, to coerce the child into sexual compliance. In intrafamilial sexual activity, the involvement violates the social taboos of family roles (Faller, 1988; Kempe, 1978).

Scope of the Problem: Incidence and Prevalence

Sexual abuse has occurred throughout every age and in every culture. It is only recently that our society has taken steps to intervene and protect children against such abuse. Freud, in the late 1800s, and Kinsey, in the 1940s and 1950s, were aware of the potential problem of sexual abuse but did not pursue in-depth studies concerning their suspicions (Finkelhor, 1979). Scholarly attention focused on the problem in the late 1960s when Vincent DeFrancis (1969) of the American Humane Association raised issues and concerns about child sexual abuse. In the 1970s and 1980s a great deal was learned about the etiology, detection, prevention, and treatment of the problem. As a result of greater understanding among health care professionals, sexual abuse is gaining recognition as a major medical and social issue.

It is difficult to ascertain the exact magnitude of the problem of sexual abuse. Studies vary in their definitions of abuse and in their means of data collection. In addition, some studies address incidence, whereas others address prevalence. *Incidence* refers to the number of new cases of sexual abuse that occur each year, while *prevalence* concerns the proportion of the population who have been victimized during childhood (Peters, Wyatt, & Finkelhor, 1986). Incidence studies rely on data reported to county, state, and national authorities and are recognized as deficient because of the large amount of underreporting to professionals that occurs in the area of sexual abuse (Finkelhor & Hotaling, 1983). Finkelhor et al. (1986) report that because of the nature of sexual abuse, "its secrecy and shame, the criminal sanctions against it, and the young age" of its victims, identification and reporting of it are discouraged, and yearly occurrence is substantially underestimated. In addition, varying levels of professional education and public awareness affect the frequency of case detection and make it difficult to judge the true scope of the problem accurately.

Prevalence studies rely on victim and offender self-reports. Because most sexual abuse goes unreported, studies that rely on large survey data from a variety of potential victim populations more accurately reflect the scope of the problem. Prevalence studies suffer from several problems. First are differences in definitions of what constitutes abuse, such as (a) inclusion of noncontact sexual abuse, described as exhibitionism and solicitation to engage in sexual activity; (b) inclusion of incidents involving peers as perpetrators; and (c) whether certain age differences constitute abuse solely because of the disparity in age between the participants. Second are differences in sample characteristics, such as (a) age of subject, (b) education level of subject, (c) ethnicity of subject, and (d) region of country surveyed. Finally, the methodological characteristics of studies differ; that is, sampling techniques vary between probability and nonprobability sampling (Finkelhor et al., 1986). A full discussion of the multiple details behind each of these topics is beyond the scope of this manual.

The Finkelhor (1979) survey of New England college students is a classic prevalence study using female and male college students from six New England colleges and universities. Finkelhor surveyed respondents concerning childhood sexual experience with older partners prior to age 17. The definition of sexual abuse used in the study included both contact and noncontact abuse with older perpetrators. Results indicated that 19.2% of the women and 9% of the men reported a sexually abusive event during their childhoods. Another student survey using similar methods and a similar population supported the Finkelhor (1979) findings (Fromuth, 1983). Based on Finkelhor's (1979) study, the prevalence of sexual abuse was approximately 1 in 5 women and 1 in 10 men.

Finkelhor, Hotaling, Lewis, and Smith (1990) report a national survey conducted by the Los Angeles Times Poll using a probability sample of 2,626 American men and women. Respondents were interviewed by phone about childhood sexual experiences and abuse. Sexual abuse was defined to include contact and noncontact sexual abuse. Findings from this random sample disclosed that 27% of women and 16% of men had been sexually abused by the time they were 18 years of age. These figures are supported by another probability sample study that was not limited to northeastern college students (Russell, 1983). These more recent data conservatively suggest that 1 in 4 women and 1 in 9 men have experienced sexual abuse prior to age 18.

The 1986 National Incidence and Prevalence Study funded by the U.S. Department of Health and Human Services reported an incidence of 2.8/1,000 cases of documented sexual abuse per year. Although this represents only those substantiated cases (cases are substantiated when either the court or child protective services determine that abuse occurred) known to child protective service professionals, the 1986 statistics reflect a threefold increase in documented cases since the initial 1980 study (U.S. Department of Health and Human Services, 1988). Based on statistical analysis and extrapolation from both prevalence and incidence studies, experts conservatively cite an incidence rate of approximately 300,000 children sexually abused in the United States per year (Krugman, 1986).

Tables 1.1 and 1.2 compare the incidence and prevalence of child sexual abuse with those of several common pediatric problems. These data suggest that sexual abuse is a hazard comparable to many familiar childhood problems.

Reports to medical and legal authorities are increasing, and professionals are becoming better equipped to identify and manage these cases. For example, in the Commonwealth of Pennsylvania in 1976 there were approximately 350 cases of substantiated sexual abuse, compared with approximately 3,000 such cases in 1984 and 6,000 cases in 1989. Table 1.3 shows a breakdown of all substantiated abuse cases over a 14-year period in Pennsylvania and highlights that more than half were cases of sexual abuse (Fleischer & Ludwig, 1988). Because evidence exists to support the notion that the actual prevalence of sexual abuse has not changed substantially over the last several decades, the data in the table reflect increased public and professional awareness of the problem of sexual abuse (Feldman et al., 1991).

TABLE 1.1   Incidence Comparison

Condition	Incidence
Leukemia/childhood cancer	2,000 cases of leukemia/year in children less than 15 years old
	6,550 cases of cancer/year in children less than 15 years old
Drowning deaths	3,200 deaths/year in children less than 4 years old
Acute diarrhea	100,000 hospital admissions/year for children
	3,000,000 ambulatory pediatric visits/year
Head injury	250,000 hospital admissions/year for children less than 15 years old
	600,000 emergency department visits/year
Sexual abuse	300,000 cases/year in children less than 18 years old

SOURCES: All figures are from *Pediatrics in Review,* as follows: for leukemia and childhood cancer, Vol. 12 (1991, p. 313; 1990, p. 5); for drowning, Vol. 10 (1988, p. 5); for diarrhea, Vol. 11 (1989, p. 6); for head injury, Vol. 12 (1990, p. 9); and for sexual abuse, 11 (1989, p. 30).

Categories Included in Sexual Abuse

The full spectrum of sexual abuse includes intrafamilial abuse, pedophilia, and rape (Kempe, 1980; Woodling & Kossoris, 1981). Intrafamilial abuse (sometimes referred to as incest) is sexual activity between individuals who are not permitted to marry, including steprelatives (Kempe, 1980). In the cases involving stepfamily relationships, the presence or absence of blood relationship is not as important as the kinship role the abuser has in

TABLE 1.2   Prevalence Comparison

Condition	Prevalence
Otitis media	70% of children will be affected, with ⅓ having repeated episodes
Asthma	10%-12% of children will have experienced signs or symptoms of asthma prior to adulthood
Syncope	15% of children will have experienced some form of syncope prior to age 18
Sexual abuse	20% of girls and 9% of boys will have experienced sexual abuse by age 18
Sickle cell disease	0.25% (1 in 400) of American black newborns will have some form of sickle cell disease (SS, SC, S-beta-Thal)
Insulin-dependent diabetes mellitus	0.25% (1 in 400) of children are affected
Cancer	0.1% (1 in 1,000) of young adults reaching age 20 will be survivors of childhood cancer

SOURCES: All figures are from *Pediatrics in Review,* as follows: for otitis media, Vol. 11 (1989, p. 133); for asthma, Vol. 10 (1988, p. 228); for syncope, Vol. 9 (1987, p. 101); for sexual abuse, Vol. 11 (1989, p. 30); for sickle cell disease, Vol. 11 (1989, p. 95); for diabetes, Vol. 11 (1990, p. 239); and for cancer, Vol. 12 (1990, p. 5).

TABLE 1.3 Forms of Abuse: Substantiated Reports in Pennsylvania, 1976-1989

Year	Number of Cases	Physical (%)	Sexual (%)	Mental (%)	Neglect (%)
1976	3,872	64.0	9.0	4.0	23.0
1977	6,183	65.0	10.0	4.0	21.0
1978	5,961	61.0	11.0	3.0	25.0
1979	4,304	66.0	15.0	2.0	17.0
1980	4,133	65.0	21.0	2.0	12.0
1981	4,689	64.0	25.0	2.0	10.0
1982	5,119	61.0	27.0	2.0	10.0
1983	5,623	60.0	33.0	1.0	6.0
1984	7,429	53.0	41.0	1.0	5.0
1985	10,993	44.0	50.0	1.0	5.0
1986	10,170	44.0	51.0	1.0	5.0
1987	10,491	44.0	52.0	1.0	5.0
1988	11,385	45.0	49.0	1.0	5.0
1989	11,780	43.0	51.0	1.0	5.0

SOURCE: Adapted from G. F. Fleisher and S. Ludwig, *Textbook of Pediatric Emergency Medicine* (2nd ed.), p. 1144. Copyright © 1988 the Williams and Wilkins Co., Baltimore. Used by permission.

relation to the child (Sgroi, 1975). Although figures on the incidence of intrafamilial abuse are difficult to ascertain, one source states that more than 90% of incest cases go unreported (Blumberg, 1978).

Pedophilia is defined as the preference of an adult for sexual contact with children. Rape is a violent act that is legally defined as forcible intercourse.

Sexual desire is not the prime motivator in most sexual offenses. Perpetrators engage children in age-inappropriate sexual activity primarily to meet nonsexual needs. Burgess and Holmstrom (1975) suggest that nonsexual motivations involve the perpetrator's need to exercise power and control. The child is an easy victim in such instances.

Conceptual Models

Sexual abuse is one form of child maltreatment not mentioned in the initial description of the battered child syndrome (Kempe, Silverman, Steele, Droegemueller, & Silver, 1962; Reinhart, 1987). Although physical and sexual abuse are frequently discussed together, there is a growing body of knowledge suggesting that they should be considered separately and viewed as separate phenomena, with unique etiologies, patterns of behavior, and treatment (Finkelhor et al., 1986; Jason, Williams, Burton, & Rochat, 1982). However, sexually abused children may experience physical abuse, just as physically abused children, although less frequently, may be sexually abused. The family dynamics that lead to sexual abuse tend to be different from those that lead to physical abuse.

Preconditions for Sexual Abuse

Finkelhor (1984) has characterized four preconditions that are typically present when sexual abuse occurs: (a) motivation of the perpetrator, (b) overcoming internal inhibitions, (c) overcoming external inhibitions, and (d) overcoming a child's resistance.

Motivation of the Perpetrator

The first precondition is that of the motivation on the part of the perpetrator. The offender experiences emotional congruence with the concept of sexual arousal related to children. Congruence may arise from prior sexual abuse of the perpetrator during his or her own childhood, from a lack of availability of alternative sources of gratification, or from the perpetrator's perception that the alternative sources are less gratifying. Motivational factors set the stage for subsequent abusive behavior if other preconditions are met.

Overcoming Internal Inhibitions

The second precondition involves the perpetrator's ability to overcome his or her internal inhibitions against committing a sexually abusive act. Although normal adults may at times become sexually aroused by children, internal codes of behavior, morals, or superego prevents them from acting on these feelings. Sexual abusers, however, overcome their normal internal inhibitions. In some cases, perpetrators may suffer from substance addictions or other forms of mental illness or instability. Such conditions may be factors in their decisions to abuse children.

Overcoming External Inhibitions

The third precondition to sexual abuse is a perpetrator's ability to overcome the external inhibitors of sexually abusive behavior. The protective environment of a family setting usually serves as a check to the victimization of a child. Abuse may occur when there is physical or emotional absence of a parent.

Overcoming a Child's Resistance

Finally, the fourth precondition for sexual abuse is the persistence of the abuser in overcoming the child's resistance to abusive acts. The abuser may use either implicit or direct coercion to impose age-inappropriate sexual contact upon the psychologically immature child. The abuser may manipulate the child and offer attention in order to ensure participation.

Characteristics of the Perpetrator

There is no definitive delineation of personality traits or specific characteristics that identify a person who is at risk for sexually abusing children. No specific set of traits exists that completely characterizes all perpetrators.

Individuality of the Nature of Sexual Abuse

Health care professionals must be careful about making generalizations, because each case of sexual abuse is unique. However, careful study of this phenomenon reveals that a number of cases occur in a fairly predictable fashion. Sexual abuse may occur as an isolated event or it may, more commonly, consist of repeated episodes over an extended period of time.

Sgroi, Blick, and Porter (1982) have described a pattern of ongoing sexual abuse that is characterized by a staged increase in contact between the perpetrator and the child victim. These researchers describe a spectrum of age-inappropriate activities that constitute sexually abusive behavior. The spectrum includes nudity, disrobing, genital exposure, observation of the child, kissing, fondling, masturbation, fellatio, cunnilingus, digital penetration of the anus, digital penetration of the vagina, vulvar coitus, intragluteal coitus, penile penetration of the vagina, and penile penetration of the anus.

Longitudinal Progression of Sexual Abuse

Sgroi et al. (1982) suggest a five-stage sequence that may characterize intrafamilial sexual abuse. The perpetrator is typically a person known to the child and family, and the child is exposed to activities that are inappropriate for his or her age and developmental level. The abuse occurs in five phases:

1. Engagement
2. Sexual interaction
3. Secrecy
4. Disclosure
5. Suppression

These concepts, described below, constitute a model for the longitudinal progression of sexual abuse.

Engagement	The perpetrator engages the child around nonsexual issues and becomes a friend or a person who provides material rewards and meets psychological needs. The perpetrator acquires access to the child and develops a relationship with him or her. The characteristics of this phase include access to the child and the development of a relationship with the child. The child may be sensitive to the threat of losing a relationship that provides attention and perceived affection.
Sexual Interaction	In the sexual interaction phase, the perpetrator engages the child in age-inappropriate sexual contact. The perpetrator manipulates the relationship developed in the engagement phase to include sexual contact. The sexual contact may progress from exhibitionism and inappropriate kissing to fondling and ultimately to oral-genital or genital-genital contact. Even if sexual interaction does not progress to fondling and genital contact, the child is still a victim of age-inappropriate sexual activity.
Secrecy	The objectives of the perpetrator are to ensure access to the child and to facilitate a continuation of sexual contact. Maintaining secrecy is essential to the perpetrator's continued access to the child. Secrecy is maintained through direct or indirect coercion. The perpetrator may use bribes or threats. The threats may be as subtle as the perpetrator's stating that he or she will disapprove of the child if the child does not comply or as explicit as threats of harm to the child or loved ones.
Disclosure	*Accidental.* Accidental disclosure occurs in a variety of ways because of external circumstances: (a) A third party observes the participants and tells someone else; (b) signs of physical injury draw outside attention to the sexual behavior; (c) diagnosis of a sexually transmitted disease or, more rarely, an injury in the genital or anal area is made; (d) pregnancy occurs; (e) nonspecific behavior changes take place, including sexually stylized behavior that is developmentally inappropriate. In accidental disclosure a crisis may occur, because neither participant decided to reveal the secret.
	Purposeful. The child consciously reveals the abusive activity. A variety of reasons exist for the child to disclose, and they may vary with the developmental level of the child. In contrast to accidental disclosure, a purposeful disclosure provides opportunity for a planned intervention.
Suppression	Once disclosure takes place, the case may enter a suppression phase. Caregivers may not want to deal with the reality of the disclosure because of denial, guilt, or fear of family disruption. The perpetrator, caregivers, or relatives may exert pressure

on the child to retract his or her account of the abusive events. The child's history may be characterized as fabrication or dismissed as fantasy.

Child Sexual Abuse Accommodation Syndrome

There are a number of factors that permit sexual abuse to continue and that prevent the child from escaping the abusive situation. Summit (1983) describes the existence of a "child sexual abuse accommodation syndrome," which includes the following behaviors or feelings:

1. Secrecy
2. Helplessness
3. Entrapment and accommodation
4. Delayed, conflicted, and unconvincing disclosure
5. Retraction

In this syndrome, the victimized child at first feels trapped and helpless. Because the child is either directly or implicitly coerced into the act, the feeling of entrapment continues as the abusive behaviors persist over a period of time. The feelings of helplessness lead to accommodative behaviors, because the child fears that no one will believe the story if he or she does tell. Such a child is usually the product of an environment that has already failed to protect. The child does not always reach disclosure and retraction. Failure to protect and support the child after disclosure only serves to reinforce the child's initial feelings of helplessness.

Long-Term Effects of Sexual Abuse

Research results on the long-term effects of sexual abuse are varied, owing to the complexity of the issues involved (Lindberg & Distad, 1985). Kempe (1980), a noted authority on child physical and sexual abuse, states that sexual abuse robs the child or adolescent of developmentally determined control over his or her own body. Individual differences in response to the trauma of childhood abusive events have been attributed to the nature of the abuse experience and individual psychological adaptation (McCann, Pearlman, Sakheim, & Abrahamson, 1988). The term *adult survivor* is used to describe persons who as adults have problems in functioning that they find are related to early damaging sexual experiences (Sgroi & Bunk, 1988). Some researchers have described a link between sexual abuse and a host of emotional and behavioral dysfunctions. Among these problems are depression, low self-esteem, suicide attempts, multiple personality disorder, school failure, regressive behavior, post-traumatic stress disorder, drug and alcohol abuse, running away, sexual promiscuity, prostitution, and delinquent behavior (Bachmann, Moeller, & Benett, 1988; Jenny, Sutherland, & Sandahl, 1986; Whitman & Munkel, 1991).

Issues of Power and Control

Studies show that sexual abuse involves more than age-inappropriate sexual contact. In many cases the heart of the problem includes the issues of power, trust, and control. Therefore, the medical evaluation of the sexually victimized patient must not become one more instance in which powerful adults impose their authority on the child's body and remove the child's control of events in his or her life. The process of taking a complete history, performing a thorough physical examination, and obtaining the necessary laboratory tests can be invasive and threatening. Therefore, the health care professional and team must convey a gentle, concerned manner and explain to the child what to expect during the evaluation. A calm, gentle, and unhurried approach will go a long way toward making the examination part of the recovery process rather than an instance of another form of assault. Awareness of the special needs of these children, along with anticipating and addressing their fears, can help make a child more secure throughout the examination process and will enhance his or her cooperativeness. When the child is uncooperative, the health care provider should not resort to force to complete the examination, but rather should address the underlying concerns of the child. This, coupled with efforts to demystify what the child will experience, will increase the chances of successfully completing an examination. The approach of the examining health care professional and the entire multidisciplinary team should be to complete the necessary medical evaluation in as nonthreatening and therapeutic a manner as possible.

In Brief

- Child sexual abuse involves engagement of a child in sexual activities inappropriate for the child's developmental age.

- Child sexual abuse frequently includes a spectrum of progressively more invasive contact occurring over a period of time.
- Reported cases of child sexual abuse are increasing, although the actual prevalence is believed to be unchanged.
- It has been estimated that 1 in 4 women (20%) and 1 in 11 (9%) men have experienced sexually abusive behavior by the time they are 18 years old (Finkelhor et al., 1990).
- The incidence of child sexual abuse, based on statistical extrapolation, is approximately 300,000 cases per year.
- One of the primary motivations of abusers is believed to be the fulfillment of nonsexual needs.
- Issues of power, trust, and control are central to child sexual abuse.
- Child sexual abuse differs from physical abuse in etiology, patterns of behavior, and modes of treatment.

2 The Evaluation

Comprehensive medical practice requires that the evaluation of any patient suspected of child abuse include a complete history, physical examination, and pertinent laboratory studies. In the case of suspected sexual abuse, the history must pay special attention to the details of the sexual victimization. Although the genital and anal examination have special importance when a sexual abuse allegation arises, this component of the examination must occur only within the context of a head-to-toe examination. Unfortunately, few primary health care providers, namely, pediatricians and nurses/nurse practitioners, are prepared for this responsibility, as evidenced by a number of articles in the literature calling for increased professional awareness of this problem and issues surrounding its identification, evaluation, and management (Gill, 1989; Horowitz, 1987; Krugman, 1986; Ladson, Johnson, & Doty, 1987; Ming, 1990; Thomas & Rodgers, 1981).

Medical schools and residency training programs provide only sparse instruction concerning the fundamentals of child maltreatment, including sexual abuse evaluation (Alexander, 1990; Dubowitz, 1988; Hibbard & Zollinger, 1990; Morrow, 1988). This is especially true in the area of the prepubertal genital examination (Herman-Giddens & Frothingham, 1987; Ladson et al., 1987). While it is not necessary to be a specialist in sexual abuse, the health care professional should be familiar with the following aspects of sexual abuse evaluation: (a) conducting an interview directed at uncovering sexual abuse; (b) performing a physical examination that includes a careful inspection of the genitalia and anus of the child; (c) collecting laboratory and forensic specimens necessary in alleged cases of sexual abuse; (d) considering a differential diagnosis of behavioral complaints and anogenital signs that may suggest sexual abuse; and (e) description and documentation of findings uncovered during the evaluation. These skills are important because cases of sexual abuse do not present only to major pediatric referral centers that have the support of a child abuse multidisciplinary team. Many cases of suspected sexual abuse present to practitioners in such diverse settings as emergency departments at general and community hospitals, urgent care centers, clinics, and private medical offices. Familiarity with the components of the evaluation and with the requirements for mandated reporting of cases of suspected sexual abuse are essential skills for health care providers seeking to provide quality care to their pediatric patients.

The sexually victimized child comes to the attention of the health care professional with diverse chief complaints. Frequently, the parent or other caregiver notices behavioral changes in the child and questions if a medical etiology exists. Through prudent questioning, the health care professional can identify children at risk and pursue a more formal evaluation for suspected sexual abuse. Less frequently, a child may be brought for a sexual abuse evaluation by a child protection service worker or a law enforcement officer following the child's disclosure.

The presenting signs and symptoms of a child who is sexually abused may include specific complaints regarding the genitalia or anus, or may be nonspecific and diffuse in nature. A child who presents with the signs and symptoms of a sexually transmitted disease obviously needs evaluation for sexual victimization with the presumption of sexual abuse until proven otherwise (American Academy of Pediatrics, Committee on Early Childhood, 1983; Centers for Disease Control, 1989). Nonspecific complaints, such as a child who suddenly develops enuresis and fear of visiting a relative's house, need careful consideration as well. The absence of an abnormal physical or laboratory examination does not rule out the occurrence of sexual abuse and does not contradict any child's story of sexual victimization (Ludwig, 1988). Table 2.1 lists examples of the types of nonspecific physical and behavioral complaints that could suggest sexual abuse.

TABLE 2.1   Nonspecific Physical and Behavioral Complaints

Physical	Behavioral
Anorexia	Compulsive or excessive masturbation[a]
Abdominal pain	Unusual sexual curiosity; repetitive sexualized play[a]
Enuresis	Excessive distractibility
Dysuria	Nightmares
Encopresis	Phobias; fears
Vaginal itching	Clinging behavior; difficulty in separation
Vaginal discharge	Aggressive behavior
Vaginal bleeding	Abrupt change in behavior
Urethral discharge	Attempted suicide
Painful defecation	

SOURCE: Adapted from G. F. Fleisher and S. Ludwig, *Textbook of Pediatric Emergency Medicine* (2nd ed.), p. 1145. Copyright © 1988 the Williams and Wilkins Co., Baltimore. Used by permission.
a. Although not specific for sexual abuse, these should be viewed as warning flags and require careful evaluation.

Approach to Evaluation of Sexual Abuse

Sexual abuse is classified primarily as a family and mental health emergency rather than a medical emergency. The nature and pattern of sexual victimization of children dictates the need for prompt evaluation and intervention, because the child may need immediate protection from further abuse (Seidel, Elvik, Berkowitz, & Day, 1986). Appropriate concern may then cause the health care professional to view the medical evaluation with a sense of urgency that may predispose the child to an inadequate evaluation. In order to assure that the child receives proper support and care throughout the evaluation, the health care professional should be familiar with the criteria for evaluation and intervention (American Academy of Pediatrics, Committee on Child Abuse and Neglect, 1991). Psychosocial support and protection take priority throughout the total examination.

Emergent Evaluation

The criteria that warrant an emergency evaluation at the time of presentation are as follows:

1. History of age-inappropriate sexual contact within the last 72 hours
2. History of acute vaginal bleeding, genital trauma, or anal injury
3. Vaginal discharge and the possibility of sexually transmitted disease

4. Possibility of pregnancy when presented with a history of penile-vaginal penetration in an adolescent who has reached menarche

If available, the multidisciplinary team should assemble to complete an evaluation when one of the criteria for emergent evaluation is present. When the examination is nonemergent, or the health care professional believes that a thorough evaluation cannot be completed, or the child is uncooperative, deferring the examination may be appropriate. If the child is uncooperative, the health care professional should attempt to identify the source of the child's anxiety and to address these fears prior to proceeding with the examination. Children who are frightened by the abuse and the evaluation may need time to develop familiarity with the health professional and the setting of the evaluation before proceeding. The complete examination may be postponed as long as referral to the multidisciplinary team and/or a follow-up visit is scheduled and provisions are made to ensure the safety of the child.

When it is necessary to defer the complete evaluation, the health care professional should use the interim time to build rapport with the child. A common fear of children is that they might be hurt when touched by a cotton swab. If this is the source of fear, the child can be sent home with cotton swabs and culturettes and allowed to practice on a doll at home.

History

The history obtained from the interview with the child is the centerpiece of the medical evaluation for suspected sexual abuse. It is perhaps the most important aspect of the evaluation. Children are unlikely to fabricate tales about detailed sexual activity (Kempe, 1978). According to Kempe (1978), the child "witnessed" his or her own victimization and describes what he or she experienced. Laypersons, attorneys, and child protection counselors often assume that physical evidence will confirm or deny the occurrence of sexual abuse. However, experience shows that the child's account of the abuse is the most important evidence to be considered in determining what occurred.

The verbal evidence that the health professional collects is vital to the protection of the child and the substantiation of suspected child abuse. The majority of sexual abuse occurs under conditions and in patterns that are not predisposed to the uncovering of physical evidence indicative of sexual abuse. The child's account of the events then becomes critical to the substantiation of sexual abuse.

The reliability of the child's account remains a controversial issue in the sexual abuse literature. Opinions vary from some who claim that children never fabricate stories of detailed sexual contact to others who claim that fabrication often occurs. A recent study examined the rate of substantiation in cases of sexual abuse in which parental conflict over custody and visitation was an issue (Paradise, Rostain, & Nathanson, 1988). Sexual abuse was substantiated in 67% of the cases identified through a chart review of patients known to an academic psychiatry practice. In this study, the investigators determined that even though substantiation of sexual abuse was less frequent in cases where parental conflict existed, there was substantiation of sexual abuse in more than half of the cases. The existence of parental conflict over custody should not detract from the need to ensure a child's safety and protection.

Physical Examination

The physical examination of a child when sexual abuse is suspected does not typically uncover physical evidence of abuse (De Jong & Rose, 1989, 1991; Finkel, 1989; Marshall, Puls, & Davidson, 1988; Woodling & Heger, 1986). A recent study of sexual abuse cases showed the presence of physical evidence in only 23% of the cases that resulted in felony convictions (De Jong & Rose, 1989). Approximately 75% of child sexual abuse is perpetrated by individuals known to the victims (Tilelli, Turek, & Jaffe, 1980), and evidence of physical force is not a common feature. The perpetrator typically wishes to avoid discovery of the abuse and avoids injuries that would raise suspicion. Many cases of sexual abuse involve multiple episodes, and there is typically a delay in reporting of the incidents (De Jong, 1985). In one study, 49% delayed reporting of the incident for at least 24 hours, and another 22% reported only after multiple episodes (De Jong, Hervada, & Emmett, 1983). Another series revealed at least a 72-hour delay in approximately 55% of cases (Rimza & Niggemann, 1982). Many children are not seen until weeks or months after the alleged abuse (Emans, Woods, Flagg, & Freeman, 1987; Woodling & Heger, 1986). If delayed reporting occurs, the superficial trauma consistent with sexual abuse may have healed, leaving no signs of acute trauma (Finkel, 1989). Woodling and Heger (1986) found that children who describe painful penetration of the vagina or anus are more likely to manifest physical findings. The discovery of findings increases in cases where a colposcope is used. Findings are more common in the context of physically violent sexual abuse, typically involving an adolescent family member or extrafamilial perpetrator (Finkel, 1988a).

Laboratory Studies

Laboratory studies bolster the findings of the history and the physical examination. The Centers for Disease Control (1989) and the American Academy of Pediatrics (AAP, Committee on Early Childhood, 1983) recommend that any child found to have a sexually transmitted disease (STD) should be evaluated for sexual abuse. Additionally, identification of seminal products on the prepubertal child is considered confirmatory evidence for sexual abuse of that child.

Documentation

The role of the health care professional includes accurate documentation of the evaluation of sexual abuse. The medical record effectively serves the interest of the suspected child abuse victim if it clearly and accurately reflects all that transpires during the interview and physical examination of the child. It is critical to keep a record of the questions asked of the child and to document the responses, noting the exact words used by the child and including a description of the affect of the child. Questions should be as open-ended and nonleading as possible. The chart must clearly differentiate statements made by the child from information related to the health care professional by the caseworker or parent. Diagrams and photographs may be helpful tools for recording diagnostic findings. The health care professional must clearly and legibly complete the medical record so that it can be used as evidence on the child's behalf. The preservation of such information is essential to a legal case at a later date.

In Brief

- Victims of child sexual abuse may present with the chief complaint of suspected sexual abuse or with nonspecific signs and symptoms.
- Specific criteria exist for the emergent evaluation.
- Medical evaluation involves history, physical examination, laboratory studies, and documentation.
- A child with an STD must be evaluated for possible sexual abuse.
- Clear documentation of the verbal and physical findings is an integral part of the sexual abuse evaluation.

3 Interview and History

The interview is the centerpiece of the sexual abuse evaluation, and serves both diagnostic and therapeutic functions. Frequently, the information elicited and documented during the history-gathering phase of the evaluation is the only diagnostic material uncovered. The interview also provides a forum for the child to give his or her own account of the abusive events to a professional who is ready to listen and provide support to the child. By collecting the history in a sensitive and caring manner, the health care professional may initiate the healing process. Ultimately, the health care provider serves the best interests of the child through careful collection of the history, documentation of verbal findings, and compliance with mandated reporting of suspected sexual abuse. The initial meeting between the health professional and the child at risk offers a unique opportunity to begin the healing process for the child and family. All contact between the health care team and the child should be nonjudgmental and characterized by concern and health promotion. Because the child needs support regardless of the outcome, the health care professional and the health care team should demonstrate a caring attitude and a willingness to act as the child's advocate throughout the evaluation.

Interview as Diagnostic and Therapeutic

A sensitive and caring manner begins with an individualized approach to the interview that is geared to the child's age, developmental level, and cognitive functioning. These variables influence the manner in which the history is approached and the way the interview takes place. Table 3.1 describes developmental issues pertinent to the history-taking effort in cases of alleged sexual abuse.

The AAP Committee on Child Abuse and Neglect (1991) has issued guidelines for the evaluation of sexual abuse in children that suggest the use of nonleading questions and a "tell me more" or "and then what happened" approach to questioning. Of course, demonstrations of shock, disbelief, or other emotions are inappropriate on the part of the interviewer.

The interview with the child is directed at uncovering specific and reliable information concerning the allegation of sexual abuse (Faller, 1990a). Questions about the abuse that deal with the who, what, when, where, and how of the situation need to be asked to allow for an adequate investigation and determination in the case. Specifically, it is essential to the evaluation effort to determine (a) what the abusive events were, (b) who was involved, (c) when the abuse occurred, and (d) where it occurred, and to gather any other relevant information. At a minimum, the health care professional should attempt to assess the child's ability to describe the sexual behavior that took place, with whom it occurred, where it happened, when it took place, and how often it occurred (Faller, 1990a). However, the health care professional must guard against interrogating the potentially victimized child. The child may already have been an object in a power and control dynamic. He or she has potentially been deprived of protection and respect by trusted authority figures. Therefore, the child may experience fearfulness during the history-taking process, because the evaluation is carried out by adults. A successful interviewer develops rapport and builds trust with the child. The interviewer should establish two-way communication, allowing the child to express him- or herself in an open way. The child's feelings about the abusive situation should be addressed in a nonthreatening, nonleading, and developmentally appropriate manner.

Although the primary goal of the interview is to collect information about the child and the abuse, the health care professional should enable the child to assume some control over the interview and evaluation. Ways in which the interviewer can encourage the child's exercise of control include (a) allowing the child to pick where to sit during the interview, (b) asking the child what name or nickname he or she would like to be called, (c) using the child's words for body parts, and (d) allowing the

TABLE 3.1 Developmental Issues in Managing the Sexually Abused Child

Age	Developmental Issues	Fears	Techniques
0 to approximately 3 years	*General:* Dependent on protection of adult Little or no ability to label time or sequence events Language only partially intelligible May not be able to identify body parts Toilet training in process *Sexual:* Normal self-exploration of genital area is pleasurable Confused if this behavior is labeled "wrong" or "dirty" If sexual abuse is not painful, it may be accepted By age 3 curious about genitals of others	Terrified of painful assault Terrified of losing protection of adult	Keep parent present during interview Use dolls to point to body parts do actions
Preschool, 3-6 years	Language skills better Able to sequence events Gender differentiation established Cannot tell time but can have established time concepts "before" or "after" *Sexual:* Sexually curious Younger children exhibit bodies Modesty develops Vocabulary of sex parts and body functions After abuse there may be masturbation, sexual play	Confused over incident Frightened by parents' anxiety and anger Feel they are "bad" for causing parents to be upset Behavior changes and phobias may develop, e.g., fear of dark, fear of strangers	Ask children to draw pictures Use doll or puppet play to note response
School age	*General and Sexual:* Sexual interest increases but usually more curious than erotic Discomfort discussing their bodies, especially outside family Extremely modest with strangers and often with parents Abusive incident may have been pleasurable and nontraumatic	Abuse is perceived as sexual, may feel "sex is wrong" Often have been threatened by adult perpetrator Guilt about what they did vs. guilt over getting adult and family into trouble Fear about their bodies, feel "dirty" or "different" after incident	Use same-sex interviewer Do not assume correct knowledge of body; a physically mature 10-year-old is not necessarily emotionally mature, or well informed Give reassurance of their non-responsibility for the abuse Give praise for having reported incident Encourage child to talk about parents' reaction Mobilize family to support victim
Adolescent	Strong urge to conform and be "normal" Knows what is and is not socially acceptable Developing body image and self-esteem is very fragile Conflict between the need to assert independence and the need for adult protection and approval	Forcible nature of sex is terrifying even to a sexually active adolescent Grief over loss of virginity Feeling that he or she is dirty or abnormal Fear of unavoidable further encounters with perpetrator Fear that a homosexual encounter may have lifelong consequences	Stress the normality of the victim—not branded for life Use charts or models Victims need to know that you have seen others with similar experiences who have recovered well Mobilize active family support Be available—give victim your phone number at work, or social worker's number Victim advocate groups very helpful

SOURCE: Unpublished data from J. Michaelson, J. Paradise, and S. Ludwig. Table adapted from G. F. Fleisher and S. Ludwig, *Textbook of Pediatric Emergency Medicine* (2nd ed.), pp. 1148-1149. Copyright © 1988 the Williams and Wilkins Co., Baltimore. Used by permission.

child to stop the interview process at any point if he or she needs a break. Forced interactions with which the child is not comfortable may be harmful to his or her mental well-being, and should be avoided.

The setting in which the interview occurs requires special attention. The privacy of the child and caregiver is the guiding principle for where the interview takes place. The interview should be completed in a quiet, private environment, free from interruptions such as ringing telephones and people opening the door. It is especially important for the health care professional in a hospital emergency room or walk-in clinic, where minimal room is usually available for confidential dialogue, to insist on a private space, because otherwise interviews may be performed in busy, high-traffic areas.

It is advisable to include other members of the multidisciplinary team, such as the clinical social worker, in the interview, to avoid distress to the child caused by his or her having to repeat the history. For purposes of legal documentation, those present in the room during the interview should be identified in the child's chart.

It takes skill and common sense to balance sensitivity with efficient fact-finding. With practice, the competent health care professional can be an effective information gatherer.

The Interview Process

The interview process consists of several phases: Phase 1 is the initial warm-up, with both the child and the child's caregiver (or caregivers) present; in Phase 2, the caregiver is interviewed; and in Phase 3, the child is interviewed. These three phases are followed by a wrap-up, with preparation for physical examination (Seidl, 1992). Each phase focuses on a therapeutic and diagnostic approach that is supportive of the child (see Chapter 7 for a discussion of the interview process in the mental health evaluation).

Phase 1: Warm-Up

During this initial meeting, the health care professional should introduce him- or herself and explore with the child and caregiver what the expectations are for the interaction. The child may be asked what he or she thinks will take place during the evaluation. The health care provider should explain the interview process and introduce the members of the multidisciplinary team who will be present during the history taking. The health care professional must inform the child in a developmentally sensitive manner of the types of questions to be asked and why the questions are necessary.

The interviewer should explain the limitations of the overall evaluation and prepare the caregiver for the possibility that a definitive answer to whether the child was sexually abused may not be possible after the initial evaluation. Finally, the interviewer should clearly explain how the disclosed information, and his or her conclusions at the end of the evaluation, will be used. Before the interview begins, the limits on confidentiality and the need to share information with agencies and law enforcement personnel should be clearly delineated to avoid feelings of betrayal on the part of the child or the caregiver.

Phase 2:
Caregiver Interview

After the initial warm-up, the child and caregiver should be interviewed separately. By talking to the caregiver first, the interviewer gives the child time to become more familiar with the surroundings and more acclimated to the setting. The child's becoming comfortable with the surroundings is enhanced if a play area is available for him or her to use while the caregiver is away being interviewed.

The purpose of the caregiver interview is to learn more about the child. It offers the health care professional an opportunity to address caregiver concerns and provides him or her a chance to educate the parental figure on the need for support of the child regardless of the outcome of the evaluation. Issues to discuss include the child's routine, supervision, development, home environment, and awareness of sex and sexuality (Seidl, 1992). Other important concerns include family structure, suspicion of abuse, social support networks, and plans for the child's future protection. The interviewer should advise the caregiver of the impact the adult's reactions and responses to the child's disclosure may have on the child. The caregiver should be encouraged to be aware of his or her own reactions to the abuse situation and to deal with the child in a manner that does not place further burden on the child.

Phase 3:
Child Interview

Although the presence of an adult ally is valuable to the well-being of the child during the physical examination, there are parts of the child's interview that need to be completed with the child alone, without a parent or other caregiver present (Faller, 1988; Seidl, 1992). The approach to the child should be one of patience and empathy. Experience in interviewing children is the key to successful collection of pertinent information about abuse. Building on what was established in the warm-up phase, the interviewer should begin with neutral/positive topics, such as school, sports and hobbies, and discussion of the child's interests (Seidl, 1987). The interviewer should reassure the child about the interviewer's motives by expressing that he or she is interested in helping children and families who come for evaluation of similar complaints and problems.

When the child and adult separate, the child may need reassurance that the adult will not abandon him or her. It is sometimes helpful to show the child where the adult will wait; in addition, it may be useful to have the caregiver leave something of his or hers, such as a coat or purse, with the child. If the child is so disturbed by separation that he or she cannot cooperate, the child may be interviewed in the presence of the nonoffending parent or adult caregiver. The adult's presence should be documented in the medical record.

Developmental/Cognitive/Language Issues

The best interviews of children occur when the health care professional can comfortably get him- or herself on the child's level, allow the child to get as close or as distant as the child wishes, and allow the child to ask extraneous or tangential questions. If the child digresses, the interviewer should allow the child to do so and then gently guide him or her back to the focus of the questioning.

The health care professional needs to draw upon his or her expertise in child development and in the known dynamics of sexual abuse in order to facilitate the child's revealing of the abuse experience. The approach of the interviewer should be nonjudgmental and nonleading. The child should be praised for his or her effort in the interview, but not for the content of what is expressed (Saywitz, 1990). Comments such as "It's hard to talk about" or "This is scary stuff to think about" may be helpful, depending on the situation, and may help the child to feel more comfortable.

The health care professional should establish a common vocabulary with the child and then use it throughout the interview. Because the child's time frame of the events may be somewhat unclear, it is helpful to date events by using holidays and other significant happenings in the child's life. The developmental level of the child should frame the types of questions asked and the approach to information gathering.

Saywitz (1990) discusses differences in language that are important to consider when interviewing children. She describes interview language in terms of being age inappropriate or developmentally sensitive. *Age-inappropriate language* is developmentally problematic for the child and potentially confusing. It includes long, complex, multiclause questions; use of the passive voice; nonspecific and confusing pronouns; double negatives; multisyllabic words; complex verbs; and hypothetical remarks. *Developmentally sensitive language*, on the other hand, includes short, single-clause questions; use of the active voice; clear use of names over pronouns; single negatives; short, understandable words; simple verbs; and direct statements (Saywitz, 1990).

The interviewer should respect the child's sense of modesty and ease or discomfort in discussing sexual behaviors. Special techniques such as the use of drawings and dolls may facilitate the child's expressing what he or she has experienced. As the use of anatomically correct dolls and drawings, and the interpretation of findings when using these techniques, requires specific training, only professionals who have such training and experience should use these aids. The findings by themselves cannot prove or disprove sexual abuse (Faller, 1988, 1990b; Goldberg & Yates, 1990; Leventhal, Hamilton, Rekedal, Tebano-Micci, & Eyster, 1989; White, Strom, Santilli, & Halpin, 1986).

Types of Questions:
Open-Ended to Closed-Ended Continuum

Faller (1990a) has developed a continuum for the types of questions that can be used in the child interview. It is based on a categorization that goes from general, open-ended, nonleading questions at one extreme to specific, closed-ended, leading questions at the other. The questioning of the child should be as nonleading as possible in order to ensure that the child is not responding to suggestions by the interviewer. Open-ended questions encourage the child to respond from personal knowledge of events rather than from the interviewer's direct or indirect suggestions (Faller, 1990a). Because the clinical interview is time-limited, the interviewer employs a mix of question types to facilitate information gathering. The interview can begin with general questions and progress to more direct questions as the details of sexual contact unfold. Faller (1988, 1990a, 1990b) describes the use of five types of questions in the sexual abuse interview: general questions, focused questions, multiple-choice questions, yes/no questions, and leading questions. Table 3.2 gives examples of these types of questions as well as a representation of the open-ended/more confident to closed-ended/less confident continuum.

Finally, sometimes even well-planned interviews may not work out. If the interview is nonproductive, the interviewer should thank the child for his or her efforts and assure the child that it is okay if he or she is not ready to talk. At that point, the interviewer should make arrangements with the child and the caregiver to see them again, or should explain to the child that he or she may want to talk to someone else who also cares about children.

Wrap-Up Session   At the conclusion of the child's interview, the caregiver rejoins the child and health care professional. This is an ideal time to make the transition to the physical examination. At this point,

TABLE 3.2 A Continuum of Types of Questions Used in Interviewing Children Alleged to Have Been Sexually Abused and Confidence in Responses (by Kathleen Coulborn Faller)

	Question Type	Example	Child Response	
Open-ended	A. General	How are you?	Sad, 'cause my dad poked me in the pee-pee.	MORE CONFIDENCE
	B. Focused	How do you get along with your dad?	OK, except when he pokes me in the pee-pee.	
		Did anything happen to your pee-pee?	My daddy poked me there.	
		What did he poke you with?	He poked me with his ding-dong.	
	C. Multiple choice	Did he poke you with his finger, his ding-dong, or something else?	He used his ding-dong.	
		Did this happen in the daytime or nighttime?	In the day and night.	
	D. Yes/No questions	Did he tell you not to tell?	No, he didn't say anything like that.	
		Did you have your clothes off?	No, just my panties.	
	E. Leading questions	He took your clothes didn't he?	Yes.	
Closed-ended		Didn't he make you suck his penis?	Yes.	LESS CONFIDENCE

SOURCE: Reprinted with permission from *The Advisor*, Vol. 3, No. 2 (Spring 1990). *The Advisor* is a quarterly publication of the American Professional Society on the Abuse of Children, Chicago, Illinois.

the health care professional should address any concerns that may have arisen during the interview process and offer support to child and caregiver(s).

Several areas of concern must be addressed. Many children and parents suspect that the child is less whole than before the abuse was identified—the "damaged goods" phenomenon initially described by Porter, Blick, and Sgroi (1982). Abused children often fear that other people are able to identify them as different. The interview wrap-up offers an opportunity for the health care professional to emphasize to the child and caregiver that, despite the physical and emotional trauma, the child is still whole and the same child as before. Because these fears are pervasive in the abused child, the health care professional can ask a general question, such as "Is anything bothering you?" or make a simple remark, such as "I see a lot of kids who have similar things happen to them, and some of them think that people can tell just by looking at them," following this with a reassuring statement that this is not the case. All children being evaluated for alleged sexual abuse need to hear, loud and clear, that they are the same children they were before the abuse. This assurance of wholeness can be reinforced during the physical examination as well.

Additionally, some parents and children have concerns about the effect the abuse will have on the child's sexuality and sexual development. The health care professional has an opportunity in the wrap-up phase to address issues of interpersonal boundaries, assertiveness, what kinds of touch are appropriate from adults and other children, and what body areas are private zones. The child should understand that he or she has the right to refuse touches that are confusing and uncomfortable. Concerns of the caregiver that the sexually abusive behaviors experienced by the child will impede or distort the child's sexuality and sexual development need to be addressed openly. Although definitive answers are not possible, the child and caregiver can be reassured that maturation will occur normally as the child continues to grow and develop in a safe and supportive environment. The family should be encouraged to enable the child to deal with his or her own fears and concerns on an ongoing basis through communication and counseling.

Sgroi (1982) points out that when a child reveals the details of abuse, the resultant turmoil of the investigation may lead the child to feel guilty and to fear that he or she should not have exposed the information to others. Because of the child's doubts and fears surrounding the disclosure of the experiences, a respected adult, such as the health care professional, should emphasize to the child that he or she did the right thing by telling about the abuse.

Compliance With Legal Responsibilities

The interview remains the central part of the sexual abuse evaluation. The health care professional must appreciate that the child's history told during the interview represents a call for help. The history may be the only evidence indicating or documenting abusive behavior, and a well-documented medical record serves to preserve this information. The health care provider is obligated, in all 50 states, to comply with statutory requirements concerning the reporting of suspected cases of sexual abuse of children. After evaluation is completed, the professional must make a decision regarding whether or not to report the case. At this point, the clinical social worker on the multidisciplinary health care team can offer invaluable contributions concerning compliance with mandated reporting requirements and, if necessary, arranging for services for the child, who may need both physical and mental protection as a result of his or her disclosure (see Chapter 7 for AAP guidelines for making reporting decisions).

In Brief

- The history-taking effort in child sexual abuse cases requires attention to the information needed as well as to the medical and psychosocial needs of the child.
- The interview can be the first step in the healing process for the child involved, if it is conducted in a sensitive and caring manner.
- The child should be given some control over the interview.
- The approach of the interviewer should vary according to the age and developmental level of the child.
- The abused child needs developmentally specific forms of reassurance that he or she is still whole and will be protected.

4 Physical Examination and Laboratory Specimens

Physical Examination

A medical evaluation of the child suspected of being sexually abused includes the victim's account of the abuse; a past medical history; a review of systems, with particular emphasis on changes in bowel and bladder habits; a thorough physical examination; and appropriate laboratory testing. In the evaluation of sexual abuse, the genitalia and anus deserve special attention, but are examined only within the context of a complete physical assessment. The examining health care professional may lack confidence in his or her ability to complete the genital examination of the prepubertal child. A number of reasons are cited for this feeling of uncertainty, including (a) inexperience during professional training in preparing children for the genital examination, (b) inadequate exposure to the spectrum of abnormal findings, and (c) failure to include the genital examination in the routine well-child office visit. This inexperience leads to unfamiliarity with the broad range of normal anatomic variants. Whatever the reason for the foreignness of such an examination, the health care professional who is uncomfortable with the examination of the genitalia will undoubtedly convey this discomfort to the patient and will have difficulty identifying healed residual of genital trauma and normal variants of anogenital anatomy.

Familiarity With the Prepubertal Examination

A study of 123 physicians, conducted by Ladson et al. (1987), demonstrated their lack of familiarity not only with conducting the prepubertal examination, but also with normal genital anatomy. The responding physicians were pediatricians (including residents) and family practitioners. In this study, 77% of the respondents stated that they examined the prepubertal genitalia more than 50% of the time, whereas 17% examined the genitalia less than 10% of the time. When asked to identify various structures on a diagram of the female external genitalia, only 59% of the 110 who attempted to label the hymen were correct. Only 61% of the 117 who attempted to label the labia majora were correct. Of the 123 who attempted to label the labia minora, only 76% did so correctly.

The results of the Ladson et al. (1987) study are of concern because 100% of health care professionals could correctly identify the eye, ear, or mouth. Few children will reveal definitive findings on examination that are residual to the alleged activities. Although acute findings of injury are readily recognizable, the chronic residual may be subtle. Thus health care professionals must improve and perfect their skills in identifying acute signs of injury, nonspecific findings, and the healed residual of genital trauma.

Laboratory Findings

The collection of appropriate laboratory specimens for the identification of STDs and forensic evidence is an important aspect of the clinical evaluation. It is included as part of the physical examination because the physical examination provides an appropriate setting for the health care professional to collect specimens when indicated. Although seminal products are infrequently found, when present they must be collected in a manner that appropriately preserves the valuable evidence. In most child sexual abuse cases, confirmation of the alleged contact through forensic evidence such as semen may be a central issue, even though identification of the perpetrator may not be in question.

Lack of Evidence

In most cases of child sexual abuse there is no physical or laboratory evidence to corroborate the child's history. It is common for most children to disclose long after the last event occurred, when physical evidence is no longer present. Lack of physical evidence alone should not lead to the conclusion that inappropriate sexual contact did not occur. Because residual to the alleged contact is infrequently present, the examiner must understand the need to be equally adept at collecting evidence through both physical and laboratory specimens and the spoken word. Throughout the examination process, it is vitally important for the examiner to anticipate and address the concerns of the child and family members prior to proceeding with the physical examination.

PREPUBERTAL ANATOMY

Basic Anatomy and Development

This section presents basic information about prepubertal anogenital anatomy, in preparation for a detailed discussion of the genital examination in the evaluation of sexual abuse. The following discussion includes two developmental staging systems. The first system, developed by Huffman (1969), consists of four stages. The stages differ according to the relative estrogen effect on the female. The second staging system, described by Tanner (1962), delineates obvious sexual characteristics, such as pubic hair and breast development in the female, and pubic hair and external genital appearance and size in the male.

An examination of the genital structures of the prepubertal female consists of the following: (a) mons pubis, (b) labia majora, (c) labia minora, (d) clitoris, (e) urethra, (f) vestibule, (g) hymen, (h) fossa navicularis, and (i) posterior fourchette. In the male, the examination includes (a) the glans and frenulum (prepuce [foreskin], if uncircumcised), (b) shaft, (c) scrotum, (d) testicle and epididymis, and (e) inguinal region, for adenopathy and hernias.

The anal examination is completed in both male and female children, with attention to (a) anal verge fissures, (b) anorectal canal, and (c) perianal region.

A bimanual or speculum examination is rarely required in the evaluation of the prepubertal child. A pelvic examination may be required in the postmenarcheal child. The focus of this manual is on the prepubertal examination.

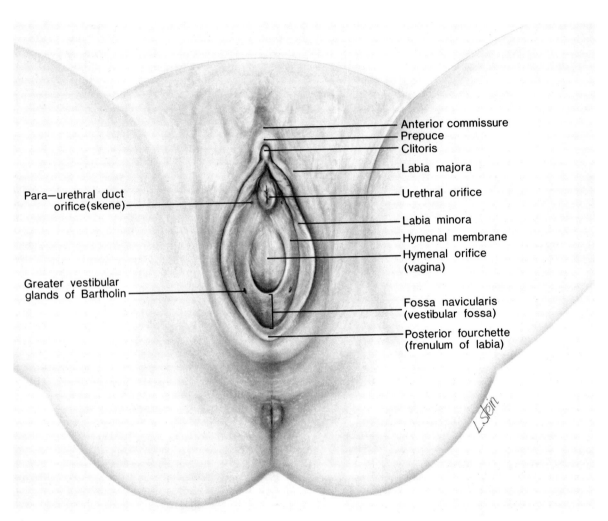

Figure 4.1
External Structures of the Female

EVALUATION OF SEXUAL ABUSE IN THE PREPUBERTAL CHILD

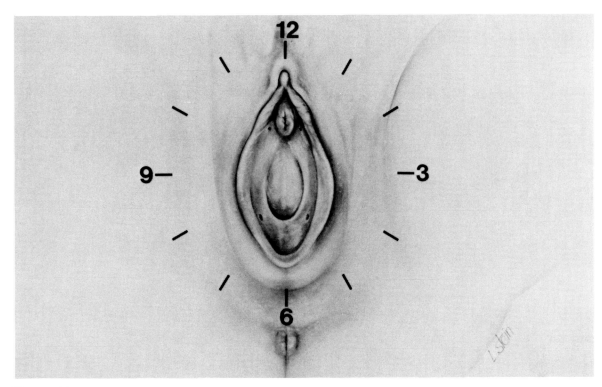

Figure 4.2
Face of Clock Orientation With Patient in Frog-Leg Supine Position

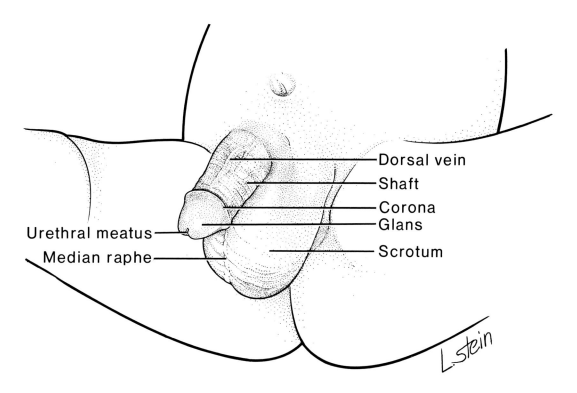

Figure 4.3
External Structure of the Male, Circumcised

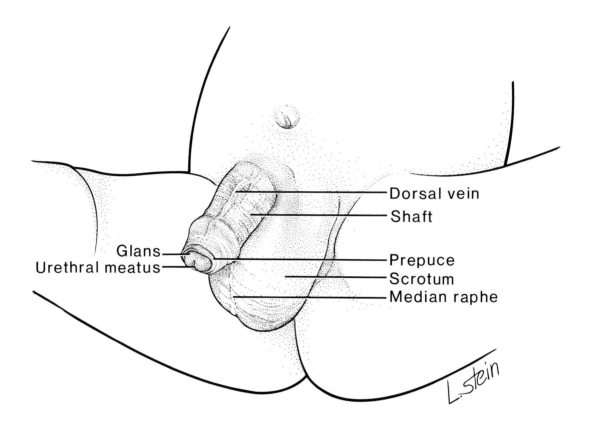

Glans —
Urethral meatus —

— Dorsal vein
— Shaft

— Prepuce
— Scrotum
— Median raphe

L. Stein

Figure 4.4
External Structure of the Male, Uncircumcised

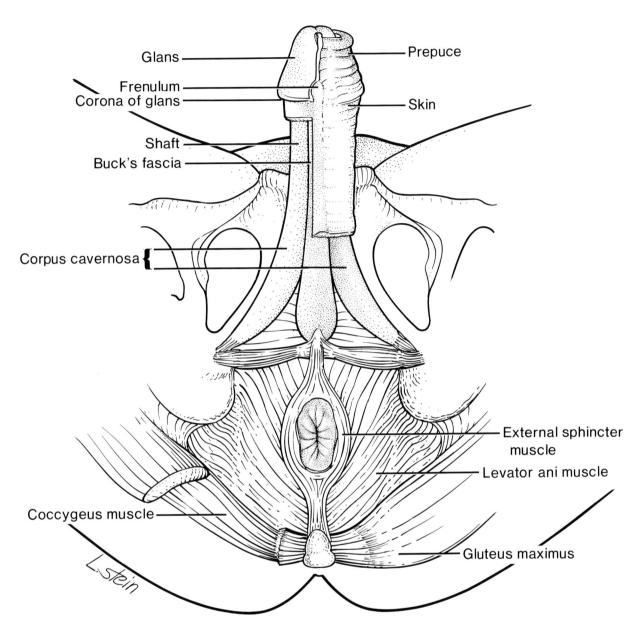

Glans

Frenulum

Corona of glans

Shaft

Buck's fascia

Corpus cavernosa

Prepuce

Skin

External sphincter muscle

Levator ani muscle

Coccygeus muscle

Gluteus maximus

L. Stein

Figure 4.5
Basic Anatomy of Male Genitalia, With Anus

Estrogen Effect on Female Genitalia: Huffman Stages

The four Huffman (1969) stages are as follows:

- *Stage 1:* postneonatal regression (0-2 months)
- *Stage 2:* early childhood (2 months-7 years)
- *Stage 3:* late childhood (7 years-11 years)
- *Stage 4:* premenarche (11 years-12 years)

Because female children grow and mature at differing rates, sexual maturity ratings more accurately reflect developmental stages than does chronological age. Huffman staging is helpful in delineating the changes that occur in the external structures of the female child on her path to sexual maturity. In Stage 1, the child's external genitalia show evidence of a profound estrogenic effect due to maternal hormones. These changes include a thick, pink, lubricated hymenal membrane. These effects recede over the first several weeks to months. At Stage 2, the female genitalia take on the immature appearance that they manifest throughout the entire stage of early childhood. At this point, there is little endogenous estrogen evident. At the end of this somewhat quiescent period, the child enters Stage 3, the late childhood stage during which the body begins slowly to increase its production of estrogen. This sets the stage for the rapid changes that are evident during Stage 4, the premenarche.

Outward Sexual Development: Tanner Stages

The Tanner stages make up a sexual maturity rating system that track the normal appearance and pattern of pubic hair in the male and female, breast development in the female, and testicle size, scrotum, and phallus development in the male. These stages provide a useful common language for communication among health practitioners. The Tanner (1962) stages are as follows.

Pubic Hair: Male and Female

- *Stage 1:* Preadolescent. No pubic hair. Fine vellus-type hair similar to that over the abdomen.
- *Stage 2:* There is the appearance of sparse, long, and slightly pigmented hair. Straight or slightly curled hair develops at the base of the penis or along the labia.
- *Stage 3:* Hair darkens and becomes more coarse and curled. It increases in density.
- *Stage 4:* Hair is of the adult type, but the area covered by it is considerably less than in the adult. No hair spread to the medial surfaces of the thighs.

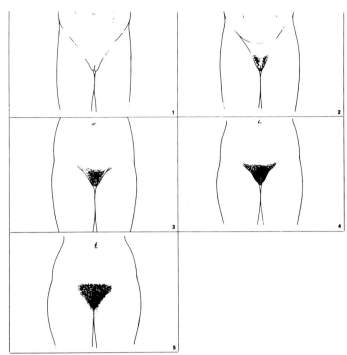

Figure 4.6
Tanner Stages: Female Pubic Hair
Reproduced with permission from Patient Care, *May 30, 1979, copyright ©*
Medical Economics Co., Inc., Montvale, N.J. All rights reserved.

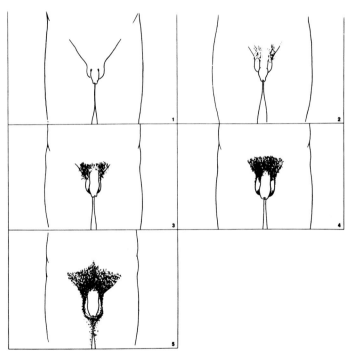

Figure 4.7
Tanner Stages: Male Pubic Hair
Reproduced with permission from Patient Care, *May 30, 1979, copyright ©*
Medical Economics Co., Inc., Montvale, N.J. All rights reserved.

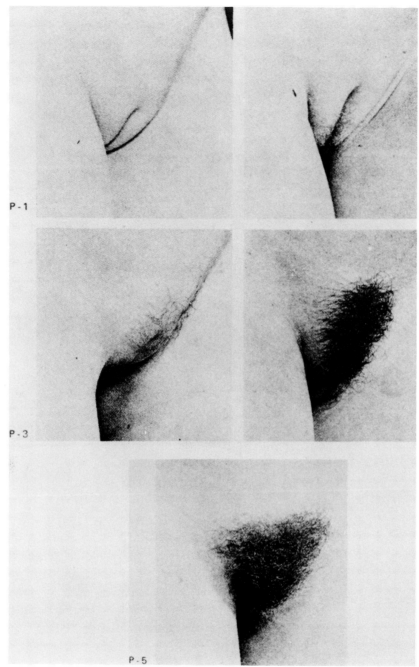

Photo 4.1
Tanner Stages: Female Pubic Hair
Reproduced from Groeidiagrammen 1965 Nederland *with permission of Wolters-Noordhoff Publishing, Groningen, The Netherlands.*

EVALUATION OF SEXUAL ABUSE IN THE PREPUBERTAL CHILD

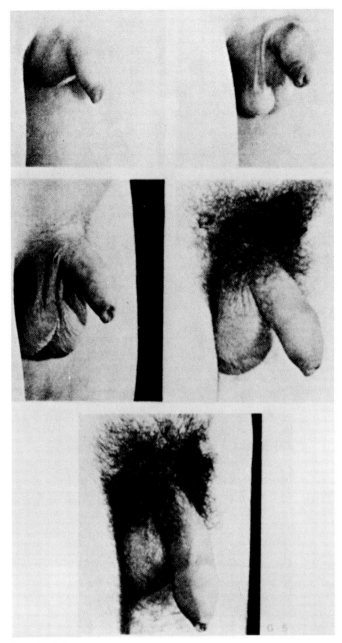

Photo 4.2
Tanner Stages: Male Pubic Hair
Reproduced from Groeidiagrammen 1965 Nederland *with permission of Wolters-Noordhoff Publishing, Groningen, The Netherlands.*

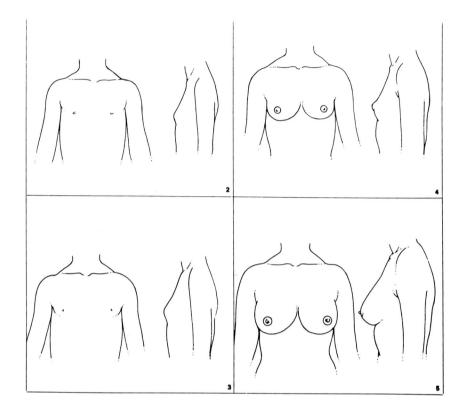

Figure 4.8
Tanner Stages: Breast Development
Reproduced with permission from Patient Care, *May 30, 1979, copyright ©*
Medical Economics Co., Inc., Montvale, N.J. All rights reserved.

- *Stage 5:* Adult hair characteristics in quantity and type. There is distribution of the horizontal pattern and hair spread to the medial surface of the thighs.

Originally, Tanner also described a Stage 6, which occurred when the pubic hair extended up the linea alba, but this has since been dropped because of its ethnic variability.

Breast Development

- *Stage 1:* Preadolescent. Elevation of papilla.
- *Stage 2:* Breast bud stage. Elevation of breast bud and papilla as a small mound with enlargement of the areolar diameter.
- *Stage 3:* Further enlargement and elevation of breast and areola, with no separation of their contours.
- *Stage 4:* Projection of areola and papilla to form a secondary mound above the level of the breast.
- *Stage 5:* Mature stage projection of the papilla only, due to recession of the areola to the general contour of the breast.

EVALUATION OF SEXUAL ABUSE IN THE PREPUBERTAL CHILD

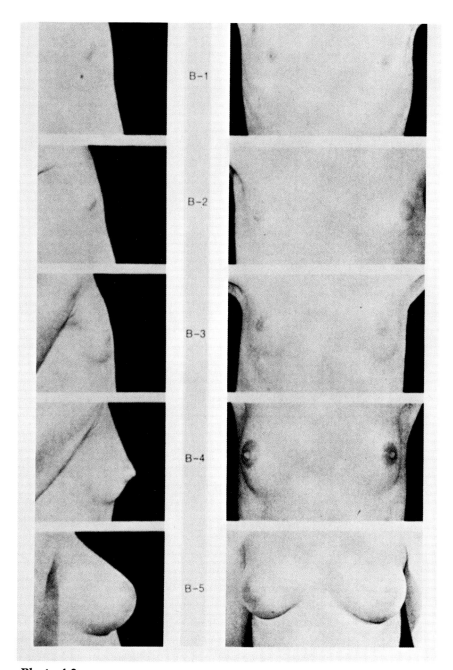

Photo 4.3
Tanner Stages: Breast Development
Reproduced from Groeidiagrammen 1965 Nederland *with permission of Wolters-Noordhoff Publishing, Groningen, The Netherlands.*

Male Genitalia	• *Stage 1:* Preadolescent. Testes, scrotum, and penis are small. Size and proportion as that in early childhood.
	• *Stage 2:* Enlargement of scrotum and testes. Skin of scrotum reddens and changes in texture. Little or no change in size of penis.
	• *Stage 3:* Further growth of testes and scrotum, with lengthening of penis.
	• *Stage 4:* Growth in breadth and development of the glans, with increased size of the penis.
	• *Stage 5:* Adult size and shape of penis.

Normal Female Genitalia

This section describes the characteristics of the normal external genital structures (vulva) within the framework of the Huffman stages. The external genitalia include the labia majora, labia minora, clitoris, bulb of the vestibule, hymenal membrane, Skene's ducts, and Bartholin's glands (Emans & Goldstein, 1982; Huffman, 1969).

Mons Pubis

The mons pubis is the skin-covered mound of fatty tissue above the pubic symphysis at the anterior commissure of the labia majora. In the neonate, the maternal estrogen effect causes the area to appear plump at birth. With the loss of maternal estrogen, the mons pubis loses its roundness. During the late childhood stage, the mons pubis begins to thicken and assume a more adult form based on endogenous estrogen production. During puberty, the mons pubis will be a site for pubic hair.

Labia Majora

The labia majora are longitudinal folds of both fatty and connective tissue that are covered by skin. This structure is analogous to the male scrotum. The labia are relatively larger and thicker at birth and remain so for several weeks to months afterward. Anteriorly, the folds are united by a commissure. Posteriorly, the folds may appear united, but in actuality they are not. If actual posterior fusion occurs, signs of actual virilization may also be evident.

In the prepubertal child, the labia majora do not completely cover the external genital structures. The labia majora change with growth. Eventually the labia of the child are completely opposed and offer protection to the other vulvar structures. During puberty, they become covered with pubic hair as well.

Labia Minora

The labia minora are thin folds of mucous membrane tissue protected by the labia majora. In the neonate, the labia minora are relatively large and may protrude beyond the labia majora.

Anteriorly, each labium divides into lateral and medial wings. The lateral labia fuse anteriorly and form the prepuce of the clitoris. The medial labia then fuse to form the clitoral frenulum. Posteriorly, the labia fuse to form the posterior fourchette. There are no hair follicles on the labia minora.

Clitoris

The clitoris is a cylindrical erectile structure that consists of a glans, prepuce, frenulum, and body. It is analogous to the penis of the male. In the neonate, the glans is disproportionately large. During growth and development, the clitoris grows at a slower pace than surrounding structures, and its relative size decreases. The glans is visible while the body extends upward toward the pubis under the skin. Clitoromegaly is a clinical diagnosis made in the prepubertal child if the length of the glans is greater than or equal to 5 mm by greater than or equal to 4 mm wide.

Urethral Meatus

The urethra forms the outlet of the urinary system, and its opening forms the urethral meatus. The urethral meatus is surrounded by several mucoid secreting glands and ducts. These are not visible normally, unless urethral prolapse is present. The paraurethral glands form an extensive network that ends in the Skene's duct. Skene's ducts are found at either side of the urethral floor. These glands and ducts do not operate until menarche, when they produce a mucoid secretion that offers protection to the urethral meatus during coitus.

Vaginal Vestibule

The vestibule is an area bounded by two structures. The lateral boundary is formed by the medial aspect of the labia minora and fourchette. The internal boundary is the anterior surface of the hymenal membrane.

Hymen

The hymen (urogenital septum) is a mucous membrane. It is a recessed structure that sits at the entrance to the vagina. The hymen has an orifice (introitus) of varying size and shape.

An assessment of the hymen includes its appearance, size and shape of orifice, relative estrogen effects, and any signs of trauma or scar tissue. The hymen is usually smooth edged and uninterrupted in the inferior quadrants. Because the hymen is estrogen sensitive, its appearance in the newborn is different and it changes as the child approaches puberty. In the prepubertal child, the external surface of the hymen and perihymenal tissues are characterized by a lacelike vascular pattern. Changes in the hymenal membrane in puberty due to estrogen result in a thickened redundant tissue that has lost its vascular appearance and takes on a pinkish-white coloration.

Because characterization of the hymen and its orifice is not standardized, there exists a great deal of controversy concerning descriptive terminology. A spectrum of variability exists in the appearance of the hymenal membrane and its orifice shape. Several clearly defined orifice configurations exist that may be further characterized by small variations. This manual refers to the fundamental hymenal orifice shapes as crescentic, annular, fimbriated, septate, cribriform, and microperforate. Other classification systems exist that are equally valid. Each of the aforementioned shapes can be further modified with the observation of clefts, bumps, notches, tags, thickening, thinning, estrogen effect, elastic character, and variability in the orifice size.

The normal size of the hymenal orifice is a contested issue. The size of the orifice may vary during the examination owing to positioning and the state of relaxation of the patient. The term *imperforate hymen* refers to a rare pathologic condition in which no orifice is present. The terms *intact hymen* and *virginal hymen* are inexact, and lead to confusion (Finkel, 1988b). As such, these terms should not be used, either in conversation or in documentation of the findings.

Fossa Navicularis

The fossa navicularis is a concave area between the posterior attachment of the hymen to the vaginal wall and the posterior fourchette.

Posterior Fourchette

The posterior fourchette is the point at which the labia minora meet posteriorly. The structure is sometimes referred to as the frenulum of the labia.

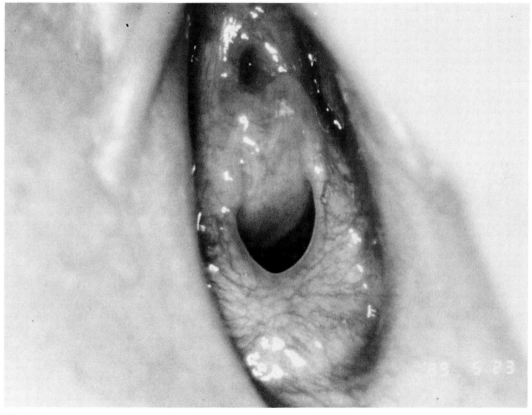

Photo 4.4
Crescentic
Crescentic-shaped hymenal orifice in a 3-year-old with slight redundancy to tissue between ten and two o'clock. Orifice edge is thin, translucent, and uninterrupted, and the external surface of the hymen has a fine, lacy, symmetric vascular pattern.

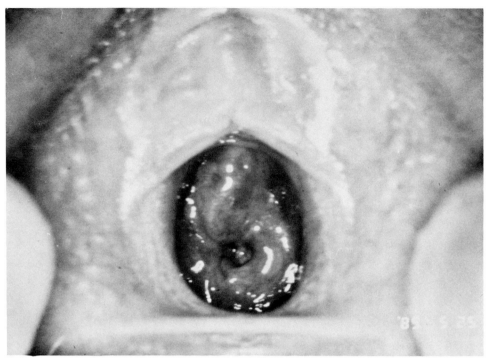

Photo 4.5
Annular
Annular hymenal orifice with redundant tissue partially obscuring the opening in a 4 9/12-year-old.

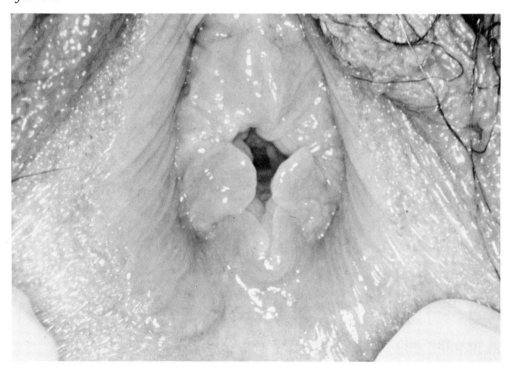

Photo 4.6
Fimbriated
A 12 10/12-year-old with a fimbriated hymenal membrane with multiple circumferential congenital clefts. Note loss of translucence and visible vascularity with onset of estrogenization.

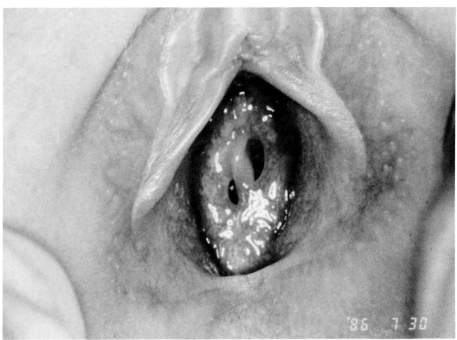

Photo 4.7
Septate

Appearance of two orifices created by a hymenal membrane septum that does not extend posteriorly in this 4½-year-old. The edge of the membrane is thin and translucent, and the external surface of the hymen has a symmetric vascular pattern.

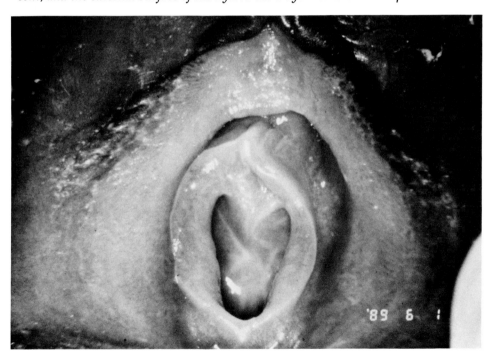

Photo 4.8
Flared

A 12 3/12-year-old with annular hymenal orifice with flared edges. Note circumferential integrity and appreciable estrogen effect.

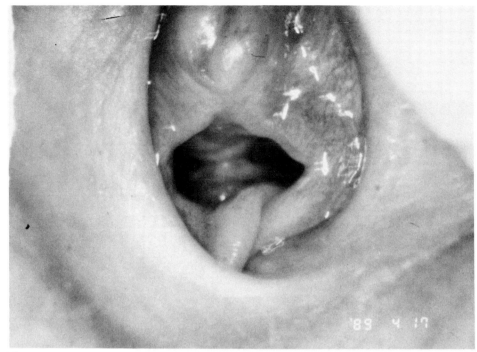

Photo 4.9
Prolapsed Hymenal Tag
Prominent prolapsed hymenal tag observed in a 6 10/12-year-old. Tag present since birth and not "fragmented" residual to genital trauma as perceived by referring health care professional.

Photo 4.10
Estrogen Effect
Estrogen's effect on the hymenal membrane of an 11-year-old results in thickening of the tissues and a loss of the prepubertal vascular pattern. The interiorly placed annular orifice is slightly obscured by redundant tissue.

Male Anatomy

The following background anatomy is offered with regard to the examination of the male external genitalia (Dodson, 1970).

Penis

The penis is a cylindrical, erectile structure composed of a glans, body and prepuce, and frenulum. The body is composed of three erectile structures, two corpora cavernosa and one corpus spongiosum. The erectile bodies are covered by thin, loosely attached skin without fatty tissue or hair, except at the base. The prepuce is a fold of similar tissue with no subcutaneous fat whose interior surface appears more like a mucous membrane. The prepuce encircles the glans and has an apical orifice that allows for retraction over the glans.

In the uncircumcised male child, the foreskin can be retracted over the glans by approximately 5 years of age. Postinflammatory adhesions may lead to phimosis of acquired etiology, making it impossible to retract the foreskin. A constricting paraphimosis may develop if the foreskin is retracted and not repositioned over the glans.

The prepuce is attached to the underside of the penis by a frenulum that contains its own artery. Circumcision involves the removal of both the prepuce and frenulum and cautery of the artery. The urethral meatus is present at the apex of the glans. The opening of the meatus may be displaced either superiorly or interiorly, in which case epispadias or hypospadias results.

Scrotum

The scrotum is a saclike structure composed of skin muscle and connective tissue. It serves to protect the testicles and associated structures. The scrotal skin is thin and elastic, and has obvious rugae. The scrotum during puberty develops a thin covering of pubic hair and increased pigmentation.

Testis

The testes are oval structures composed of a compact array of tubules, connective tissue components, hormone-secreting cells, and sperm-producing cells. Testicles are readily palpated through the thin skin of the scrotum. In the normal male, both testes are descended and palpable. The right testis generally hangs lower than the left owing to the fact that the arterial supply to the left testis comes from the renal artery, as opposed to the aorta.

In young children, an unusually brisk cremasteric reflex causes a "retractile" testis. A retractile testis is descended but difficult to palpate. Undescended testes imply abnormal gonadal development. In such cases, the testes must be surgically approached to avoid infertility and possible undetected testicular cancer in the future.

Epididymis   The epididymis is a long, narrow, tubelike structure that carries sperm from the testicle to the seminal vesicle. It is composed of a head, body, and appendix. The epididymis may be palpated through the thin skin of the scrotum until it enters the inguinal canal. Inflammation of the epididymis is called epididymitis.

Anal Anatomy   The anus is the opening of the rectum through which feces are extruded. The opening is surrounded by both internal and external sphincter mechanisms that collectively make up the anal sphincter. The tissue that overlies the external anal sphincter is referred to as the anal verge. This loose cutaneous tissue extends back to the pectinate line (see Figure 4.9), where the anal papilla and columns interdigitate with the anal verge tissues. The external anal tissues generally have a symmetric appearance of circumferentially radiating skin folds known as rugae. The typical perianal appearance on examination is of a symmetric, pigmented, puckered mucus membrane that has a natural tone and reflexively tightens when the buttocks are separated. During puberty, coarse pubiclike hair surrounds the pigmented tissue in both males and females.

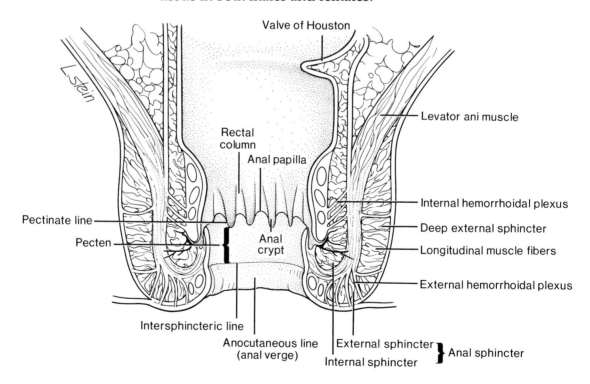

Figure 4.9
Anal Anatomy

FINDINGS IN SEXUAL ABUSE

Variables Affecting Physical Evidence

The child's verbal description of the abuse that occurred should serve as a guide in the examiner's search for physical findings. When physical findings are present, they may help to confirm the alleged inappropriate contact. However, the professional must remember that the absence of such findings does not deny the occurrence of abuse, as many activities would not be anticipated to have residua. The child may disclose only a portion of the details of his or her abusive experience(s). Therefore, it is imperative to assume that more has occurred than disclosed, and a complete examination of the child is always indicated.

A number of variables may affect the likelihood of finding physical evidence of sexual abuse, such as the following (Finkel, 1988a):

1. Use of force, or absence of such
2. Age difference between child and perpetrator
3. Size of object introduced into body orifice
4. Level of resistance by the child
5. Use of lubricants
6. The specific abuse activity
7. Position of the child during the victimization
8. Chronicity and acuity of the abuse

Findings in Sexual Abuse

This section focuses on the findings that may be noted in cases of acute or chronic sexual abuse. Although many children will not complain of injury or present with signs or symptoms suggestive of STDs, there are certain characteristics to consider in differentiating inflicted trauma from the infrequently seen accidental injuries to the genitalia (De Jong & Rose, 1989; De Jong, Weiss, & Brent, 1982; Finkel, 1988b; Josephson, 1979).

The manner in which children are engaged in sexual contact helps to explain why residual findings as a result of physical force and restraint are unusual in child sexual abuse. This occurs in part because the perpetrator has little intent to harm the victim physically while engaging the child in sexual contact.

Sexual abuse often follows a pattern of ever-increasing contact between perpetrator and victim. By not harming the child, the perpetrator hopes to ensure the continued cooperation of the child. Both implicit and explicit threats and rewards are utilized to maintain secrecy around the events. Physical injuries requiring medical attention could lead to disclosure and discovery. Most injuries that do occur are superficial and heal without residual findings, because most children disclose long after the last contact and are well beyond the 72 to 96 hours necessary for superficial trauma to resolve (Finkel, 1989). In addition, more serious injuries can heal with unanticipated residual findings based on the initial appearance of the acute injuries. The retrospective interpretation of such residual findings can be difficult without knowledge of the premorbid state. Physical force is more common in cases that involve adolescents or perpetrators unknown to the victim (Finkel, 1988a). In such cases, extragenital, genital, and perianal findings may be more easily identified, and their cause obvious.

Degree of Physical Contact

The legal definition of *rape* includes the act of sexual intercourse, although the specifics may vary from one state to another. A strict legal dictionary definition states that any penetration between the labia constitutes rape, no matter how slight. In some situations, the child is exposed to inappropriate stimuli without actual physical contact. Abuse situations may include a child being exposed to an adult's genitals or observation of an adult stimulating him- or herself. In such cases, there would be no physical findings on the child. Children exploited for pornographic purposes may also escape physical contact.

Extragenital Trauma

Frequent sites for extragenital trauma include breasts, extremities, neck, buttocks, and oropharynx. These findings may represent residual to the use of force and restraint. Ligature marks and traction alopecia are additional signs of restraint and force. The health care professional should document all abrasions, lacerations, contusions, and bite marks. Documentation is most complete when diagrams or photographs of the findings are included in the report (Ricci, 1991). The medical record must also provide a clear explanation of the examination findings to support any photographic documentation. Thus if photographs fail to develop properly or are otherwise unsatisfactory, written documentation remains.

During a complete physical assessment of the child, the health care professional should look for signs of (a) trauma, (b) sexually transmitted disease, and (c) forensic evidence such as the perpetrator's pubic hair and semen.

Fondling and Digital Penetration

In situations where the primary activity of the perpetrator involves fondling of the child's genitals, the degree of force employed will be a prime determinant of the findings. Commonly, no physical findings exist because the primary objective of the perpetrator does not usually include inflicting pain on the child. When increasing force is utilized, findings may include erythema of the fondled area, edema, superficial abrasions, and contusions.

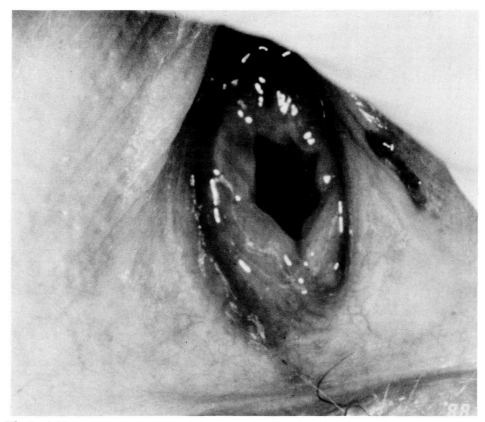

Photo 4.11
Findings in Digital Penetration
Diffuse erythema and laceration to edge of hymenal membrane at six o'clock position in this 9 7/12-year-old are secondary to digital penetration.

As the level of abusive contact increases, the perpetrator may forcefully introduce fingers or objects into the vagina or anus. In such cases, significant findings may include lacerations to the hymen and vaginal wall. If abusive activity is ongoing, the findings may progress from the acute to a more chronic picture. Findings in chronic abuse may include alterations in the contour of the hymenal membrane orifice, healed transections, and post-inflammatory labial agglutination. Clinically, genital and hymenal injuries between the nine and three o'clock locations (with the child in the supine frog-leg position) occur more frequently in fondling and digital penetration, as the finger enters over the mons pubis between the labia minora and is rubbed over the urethral meatus. In the context of fondling/digital penetration of the vagina or anus, superficial laceration may result from the perpetrator's fingernails. However, under most circumstances there is little residual to fondling, and the residual is nonspecific when present.

A history of dysuria following fondling may help corroborate the child's story. This history indicates periurethral trauma

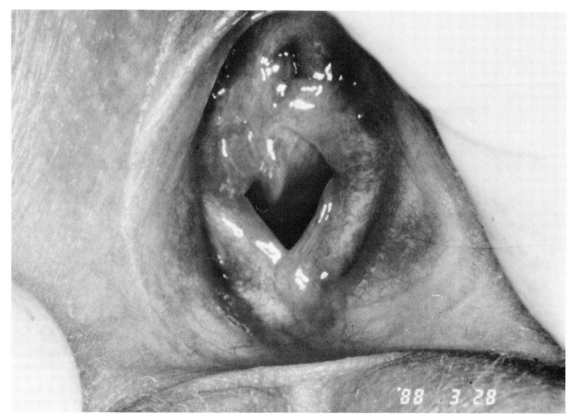

Photo 4.12
Findings in Digital Penetration
Diffuse erythema and two interruptions in the integrity of the membrane edge at two and ten o'clock in this 8 9/12-year-old are secondary to digital penetration.

EVALUATION OF SEXUAL ABUSE IN THE PREPUBERTAL CHILD

and not urinary tract infection. The findings are admissible in court if the historical details are obtained in a manner that is nonleading and meet all the criteria for exceptions to hearsay rules (Finkel, 1992). In general, dysuria in cases of sexual abuse is infrequently associated with a documented urinary tract infection (Klevan & De Jong, 1990).

Male Abusive Findings

In the male child, fondling of the genitals may result in edema or abrasions on the shaft, glans, and foreskin of the penis, or on the surface of the scrotum or perianal area. The severity of the abrasions usually depends upon the degree of force the perpetrator uses. Occasionally, bite marks will be evident on the penis.

Anal Examination Findings

It is difficult to interpret residual findings from the introduction of a foreign body such as a penis, digit, or other object into the anus, particularly when no acute signs are present. The external anal sphincter has the ability to dilate significantly to pass large stools without any obvious injury to the sphincter or anal canal. Therefore, depending upon the age of the child, the size of the object introduced, the degree of force, cooperativeness of child, and the use of lubricants, there may or may not be any residual findings from the repeated introduction of an object into the anus. Because most perpetrators have little intention to harm the child physically while introducing an object into the anus, it is most likely that only superficial and nonspecific signs will be noted when the injuries are acute. These superficial injuries may include rectal fissures, chafing, and erythema. More significant acute injuries may include bruising, lacerations, edema, and posttraumatic hemorrhoidlike tags. The most serious acute injuries include complete transection of the external anal sphincter, laceration, and perforation of the rectosigmoid. Any anal tears that extend onto the perineum should not be considered to have occurred from passing hard stool.

Perianal venous congestion and changes in pigmentation of the perianal tissues alone should be cautiously interpreted and are insufficient to confirm sodomy.

No experimental models exist to assess the effect of repeated introduction of a foreign body into the anus of a child. Thus the question of how often and how much force is necessary to cause the changes noted from chronic sodomy or digital penetration is difficult to answer. Clinical experience suggests that when an object is repeatedly introduced into the anus, the following may be seen: (a) loss of fine symmetric rugal pattern, with replacement by hypertrop; (b) anal scars as the healed residual to significant acute injuries; (c) loss of subcutaneous fat; (d) decrease in sphincter tone; and (e) abnormal response to traction of external anus when rectal ampulla is free of stool. All of these findings when present must be corroborated with an appropriate history.

Nonspecific findings, such as erythema, perianal excoriation, and pigmentary changes, require an appropriate history and should be contemporaneous with the alleged contact to be considered indicative of abuse. Diagnostic findings include serious injuries such as transection of the anus, perianal scarring, perforation of the rectosigmoid colon, and the recovery of seminal products from the anorectal canal, with or without signs of acute or chronic trauma.

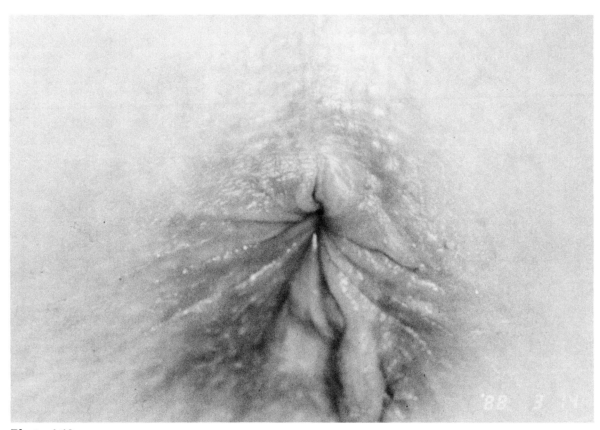

Photo 4.13
Loss of Rugal Symmetry
Asymmetry of rugal pattern most evident at five o'clock position, with tag and scar tissue at five through seven o'clock positions.

EVALUATION OF SEXUAL ABUSE IN THE PREPUBERTAL CHILD

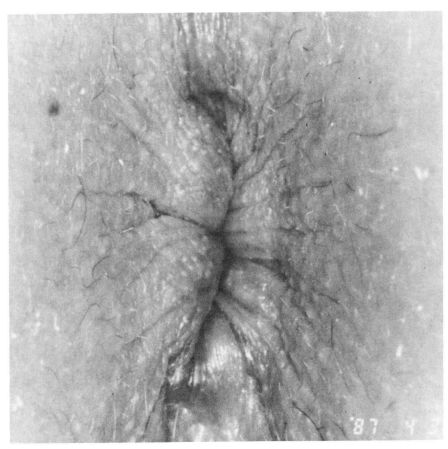

Photo 4.14
Loss of Rugal Symmetry
Asymmetry of rugal pattern resulting in hypertrophied rugae. This 9 7/12-year-old girl was subjected to repeated penile-anal penetration.

Penile Contact With Genitalia and Anus

Characteristic findings may result when the abuse involves penile contact without introduction of the penis through the hymenal orifice or into the anorectal canal. Vulvar coitus occurs when the perpetrator's penis is placed against the child's vulvar structures. In such abuse, trauma may result to the anterior commissure, posterior fourchette, medial aspects of labia minora, and possibly to the external surface of the hymenal membrane. Acutely, lacerations, abrasions, erythema, and edema may result. On a chronic basis, subtle scar tissue in the posterior fourchette or on the external surface of the hymen may occur. In vulvar coitus, the perpetrator may ejaculate on the child's abdomen or within the intracural region. Seminal products should be looked for if a history of ejaculation is provided. Children will frequently state that an object has been placed inside them,

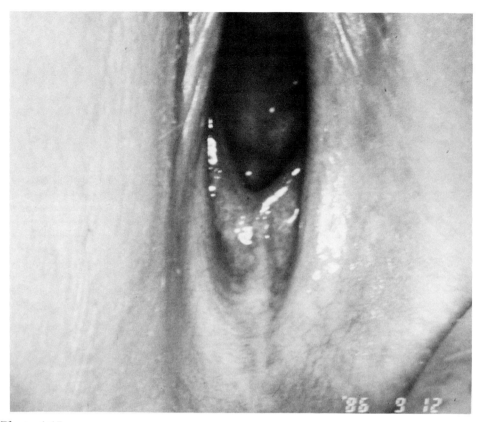

Photo 4.15
Penile Stimulation Without Penetration
Healed laceration to fossa navicularis and posterior fourchette is the result of forceful vulvar coitus. Note midline interruption of normal vascular pattern.

and yet no confirmatory physical findings are present. This situation should suggest to the examiner that the child experienced vulvar coitus even though the child's perception may have been different.

Intragluteal "coitus" occurs in the male or female victim when the penis is placed between the gluteal folds. The friction of the penis over the surface of the external anal verge tissues between the buttocks may result in edema, contusions, and abrasions, involving the natal cleft, perianal, and anal tissues.

In cases where rubbing of the perpetrator's penis on the child has occurred, the examiner should assess for the presence of seminal products on the back and buttocks. Pubic hair and other trace elements (e.g., fibers) may also be found on the child's body. In any case where the perpetrator has direct genital contact with the child's body or indirect contact through genital secretions, there exists the possibility of acquiring sexually transmitted diseases.

EVALUATION OF SEXUAL ABUSE IN THE PREPUBERTAL CHILD

Oral-Genital Contact

In cases where a history of oral-genital contact has been provided, there are some specific findings that may be present. The child forced to perform fellatio may have petechiae of the palate or posterior pharynx. Tears to the labial frenulum may result as well. Depending on the time lapse since the last episode of abuse and occurrence of ejaculation, the evaluator should look for evidence of seminal products in the oropharynx and nasopharynx.

If the perpetrator performs fellatio or cunnilingus on the child, possible acute signs would include petechiae, abrasions, or bite marks to the genitalia, depending upon the time interval between the contact and the examination.

Penile Penetration

Depending on the child's age, penetration of the vagina by a penis may or may not lead to significant findings. The findings

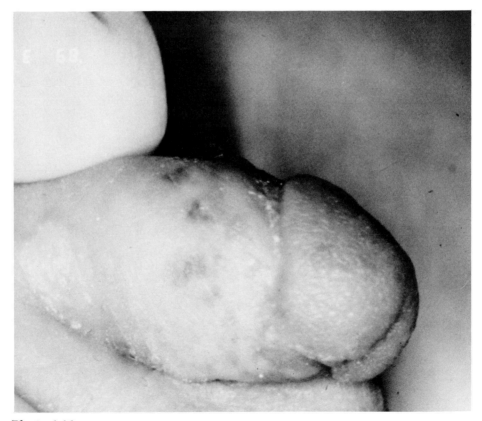

Photo 4.16
Penile Trauma
Circumferential bite marks to body of penis.

depend on a number of variables that militate for or against residual. It is expected that the introduction of an adult penis into a prepubertal child's vagina should acutely produce obvious signs of trauma. This is true if the abuse is acute and forceful.

In cases of long-standing abuse in which progressively more invasive contact occurs over time, the hymenal membrane orifice may be progressively stretched, with gradual widening and enlargement of the orifice to the point that the eventual introduction of a penis may be possible with minimal residual findings. Lubricants, as well as cooperation on the part of the child and delayed disclosure of the events, reduce the likelihood of identifying the acute residual to sexual contact. In such cases, the child's account of the abuse may be the only evidence, as clinical experience confirms that superficial genital injuries heal rather quickly and healing can be complete in 10 to 14 days with little or no residual (Finkel, 1989).

Hormonal factors may add to the difficulty in interpreting the residual to suspected sexual abuse. Rising estrogen levels, as described in Huffman's staging, will alter the appearance of the prepubertal child's genitalia. This will lead to progressive

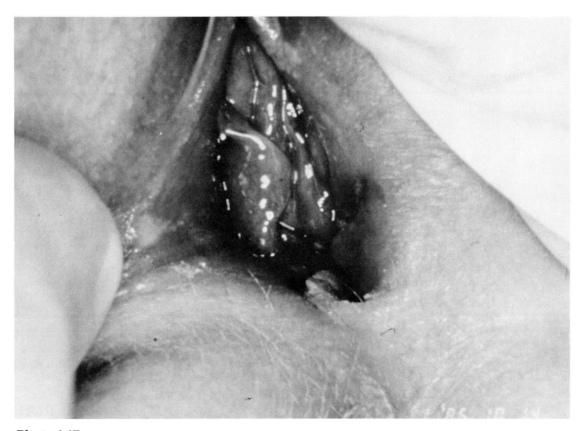

Photo 4.17
Penile Penetration
Tissue edema, ecchymosis, and laceration to hymenal membrane, vaginal wall, and posterior fourchette following penile penetration of the vagina of a 19-month-old.

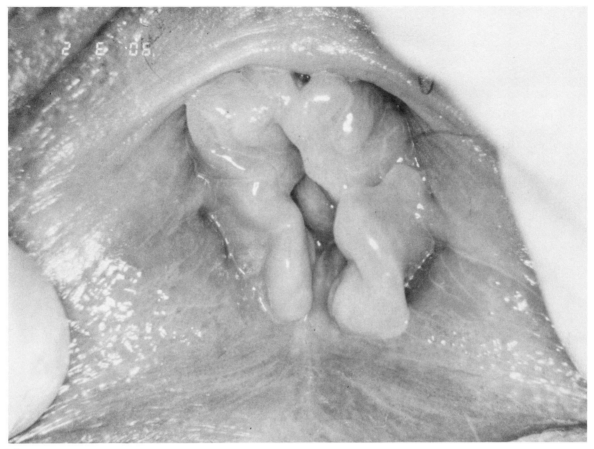

Photo 4.18
Penile Penetration
A 12-year-old in lithotomy position. Estrogenized hymenal membrane with prominent interruption in the integrity of the hymenal membrane at the six o'clock position that extends to the vaginal wall. Scar tissue present at the base of the laceration. Remainder of hymenal membrane reveals redundant tissue with a defect at the three o'clock position

changes in the thickness, redundancy, elasticity, and vascular pattern of the hymen and related structures as the child approaches menarche. Redundancy and thickening of the hymen secondary to estrogen effect may alter the appearance of preexisting trauma and make residual findings quite subtle and difficult to identify. The elasticity of the membrane in the pubertal child may afford the intromission of a penis with surprisingly little residual.

The findings of sexual abuse may be subtle or may mimic conditions not normally thought of as indicative of sexual abuse (see Chapter 5). For example, one case report describes the finding of an imperforate hymen as a sign of sexual abuse (Berkowitz, Elvik, & Logan, 1987b). Another describes fine white scar tissue in the posterior fourchette as well as labial adhesions as the finding in several sisters abused by male relatives (McCann, Voris, & Simon, 1988).

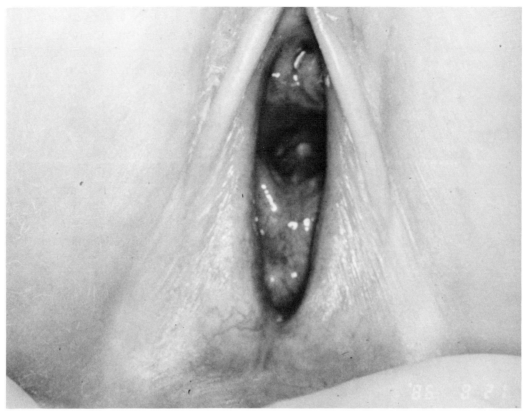

Photo 4.19
Example of Subtle Findings
A 6½-year-old with healed laceration extending across posterior fourchette; initial injury sustained during vulvar coitus. Note hypopigmented character of scar. Attenuated edge of membrane between four and eight o'clock secondary to repeated digital penetration. Patient in knee-chest position.

Summary of Abuse Findings

Acute findings of injury, whether noted in the genital or anal area, are erythema, edema, abrasions, lacerations, and bruising. As acute injuries heal, they may leave little or no residual findings. This makes the retrospective interpretation of changes in anogenital anatomy difficult. For example, differentiating changes in the appearance of the edge of the hymenal membrane may be difficult if an acute laceration is not present. Laceration will result and most likely extend to the posterior vaginal wall when a large-diameter object is forcefully passed through a smaller-diameter orifice. This finding is diagnostic of trauma when observed in the posterior quadrant of the hymenal membrane. However, a smaller-diameter object passed through a larger orifice may not tear the membrane, or, if it does cause a tear, the tear may not extend to the vaginal wall. Smaller interruptions in the edge of the hymenal membrane that do not extend to the

EVALUATION OF SEXUAL ABUSE IN THE PREPUBERTAL CHILD

posterior wall may be difficult to differentiate from congenital clefts. Penetration injuries most commonly result in changes to the hymenal membrane in the most posterior portion and may include injury to the fossa navicularis and posterior fourchette. The presence of scar tissue involving any or all of the following structures must be presumed to be of traumatic origin: (a) labia minora, (b) hymenal membrane, (c) fossa navicularis, (d) posterior fourchette, and (e) anus. A history concerning such injuries must be sought. When vulvar coitus occurs, the pattern of acute injury may involve the medial aspects of the labia minora, the posterior fourchette, and the periurethral area. Fondling of the genitalia, with the finger contacting the mons pubis and rubbing the superior aspects of the labia minora inferior to the clitoral hood and over the external urethral meatus, may result in localized redness, abrasions, and edema. However, no chronic residual findings may be apparent and only a history of postfondling dysuria may be obtained to corroborate the event. Rarely, an

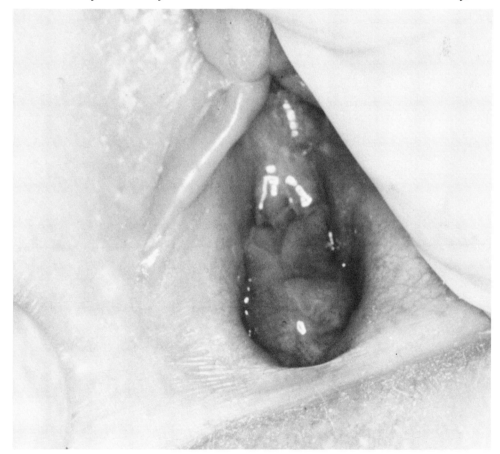

Photo 4.20
Effect of Examining Position and State of Relaxation on Hymenal Orifice Size
A 4½-year-old girl examined in supine frog-leg position. The orifice is not visualized in this position owing to contraction of pubococcygeal muscle and redundancy of surrounding hymenal tissue. (See Photo 4.21.)

object introduced into the vagina may perforate through the posterior fornix and enter into the peritoneal cavity.

Hymenal Orifice
Controversy exists over the relevance of the size of the hymenal orifice. The size of the hymenal opening can vary with the degree of traction placed on the labia majora and the degree of relaxation of the child during the examination. The age and pubertal development of the child may also affect the size of the hymenal opening (Heger & Emans, 1990; McCann, Voris, Simon, & Wells, 1990). The diameter of the hymenal orifice alone should not be used as a screening test for the presence of sexual abuse. The hymenal diameter may be helpful in specific cases, but no generalization can be made.

Anal Penetration
See the above section on anal examination findings for a related discussion.

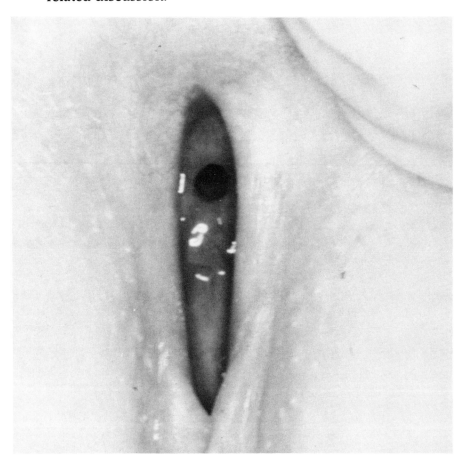

Photo 4.21
Effect of Changing Position
Child from Photo 4.20 placed in prone knee-chest position. Gravity allows redundant tissue to fall forward, and a 3-mm annular hymenal orifice is now visualized. This child demonstrates the variability of hymenal orifice based solely on positioning and relaxation.

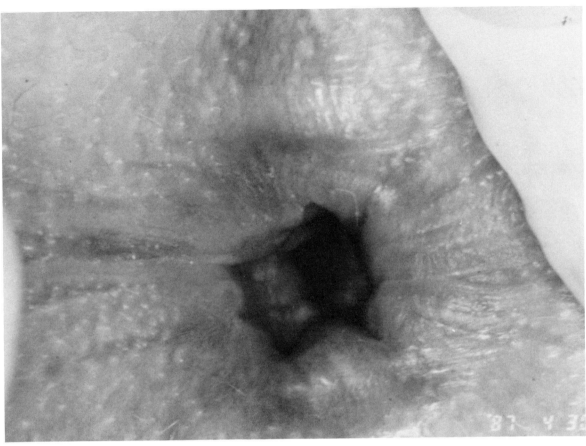

Photo 4.22
Penetration of Anus
With gentle separation of buttocks in this 9 7/12-year-old girl, anus noted to be dilated and to have appearance of decreased sphincter tone. No reflex tightening when buttocks are separated; patient reports frequent anal penetration by perpetrator.

Accidental Trauma

The most common type of accidental injury involving the genitalia is the straddle type. Straddle injuries occur when the child's soft tissues are crushed between the pubic bone and a hard object. These injuries are typically seen after the child falls on a bicycle crossbar, balance beam, or jungle gym. It is highly unlikely that such an accident could damage the recessed hymenal membrane (Finkel, 1988a). Trauma to the hymenal membrane may result from an accidental impaling injury or from an object purposefully directed at the membrane. Some examiners will be surprised at the extraordinary explanations that may be provided to account for genital injuries (see Chapter 5).

At present, there is no scientific evidence to support the common belief that girls injure their hymens during activities such as horseback riding, gymnastics, and tree climbing (Finkel,

1988a). Furthermore, little is known about the changes to the anogenital anatomy that result from masturbation (Schoon, 1988). Clinical practice supports the belief that self-inflicted injuries, especially in the context of masturbation, are exceedingly rare unless the child is psychologically impaired (Bays & Jenny, 1990). Accidental injuries to the anus are also extremely unlikely.

THE PHYSICAL EXAMINATION

Preparing for the Physical Examination of the Child

Minimal prerequisites of a thorough examination of a child suspected of being sexually abused are time and patience. The examiner must understand that the child will most likely have an inaccurate preconception of what the physical examination entails. Prior to proceeding, the examiner must address all concerns of the child in order to reduce preexisting fears and thus improve the potential for cooperation throughout the examination.

Taking the time to explain the importance of the evaluation helps to earn the child's confidence and trust and sets the stage for the physical examination and the collection of laboratory specimens. The rapport developed with the child during the interview will serve the examiner well as the examination proceeds. No coercion, deceit, or force should be utilized, either directly or indirectly, to convince a child to submit to an examination of his or her body and genitals. The child must be fully informed and cooperative. Under no circumstances should an uncooperative child be physically restrained for an examination. These children are already victims of the abuse of authority and control and should not be subjected to overwhelming force during a medical evaluation. In the unlikely event that an emergent evaluation is essential for the child's well-being and the child is unable to cooperate with the examination, use of anesthesia may be necessary. Coerced examination represents yet another assault to the child and demonstrates an abuse of the adult clinician's position of authority.

Because abused children have had little or no control over what they have experienced, once disclosure occurs it is important for these children to begin to take control over what is happening to their bodies. Allowing the child to have choices, such as where to sit during the examination—in an ally's lap, in a chair, or on a table—or who is to be the adult ally present during the examination, helps give the child some control. Such gestures build confidence, provide the child with options, and may have considerable therapeutic value. In addition, the examiner may give the child a choice as to which gown he or she would like to wear. The child should keep on socks and underwear until the examination requires their removal. The examiner should honor the requests of the child and answer questions as they arise during the evaluation.

Tools of the
Physical Examination

The examination depends on inspection and gentle palpation to expose various structures. In most cases, the prepubertal child can be examined without sophisticated instruments. An examination area with good lighting and a hand-held magnifying lens are usually all one needs to perform a thorough examination. An external inspection of the hymenal membrane and perihymenal tissue is generally sufficient. Use of a vaginal speculum in the prepubertal child is rarely necessary unless trauma to the hymenal membrane suggests that an object was placed through the orifice and intravaginal trauma is suspected. If a foreign body is suspected, irrigation of the vagina with sterile distilled water using a soft feeding tube generally is successful in dislodging the material, and the use of instrumentation and concomitant use of anesthesia for such a procedure can be avoided. In the prepubertal child, toilet tissue is a common foreign body.

In some centers, a colposcope is available and utilized in the examination. This instrument, initially used for the visualization of the cervix, now can be used to assist in the visualization of external genital structures as well. The colposcope provides an excellent light source, magnification, and, when attached to a camera, the ability to document the examination through either 35-mm photography or videotape. The colposcope is noninvasive and can be made nonthreatening to the child when appropriately introduced.

Method of
Evaluation

A general physical examination should be performed in the typical head-to-toe manner. The reason for incorporating the genital and anal examination in the context of a complete evaluation is to make a statement to the child that all parts of his or her body are important. In addition, the genital and anal examination may be threatening to the child, so proceeding through the other parts of the examination may be helpful in the transition to the genital and anal examination. It is necessary for the examiner to take time to explain to the child what will happen and to answer any questions the child may have.

The health care professional should pay special attention to any signs of physical abuse or neglect when completing the general physical examination. Physical evidence of injury should be adequately documented with diagrams, photographs, and descriptions in the medical record. Authorities disagree on the proportion of sexual abuse cases that have concurrent extragenital trauma. Extragenital trauma such as grasp marks, ligatures, and bite marks reflect the use of force or restraint. De Jong, Hervada, and Emmett (1983) report approximately 10% in their study, and Rimza and Niggemann (1982) report 16% in their review. Owing to the nature of the abusive event, children abused by strangers have a higher incidence of physical trauma compared with those abused by perpetrators who are known to them. When reasons exist to suspect the presence of semen, the body surface should be examined for evidence of semen or other body fluids. A Wood's lamp is helpful, because semen may fluoresce.

Attention to the oropharynx is necessary because orogenital contact may be suspected or described. The examiner should observe for evidence of trauma, including palatal petechiae and tearing of the delicate labial frenulum. Under most circumstances, there is no residual when a child is forced to engage in orogenital contact.

Whenever possible, a mental health professional should be involved from the beginning of the investigation, because the primary impact of sexual victimization is psychological. A mental health professional can assist in determining the impact of the victimization and the best therapeutic approach (see Chapter 7, Mental Health Evaluation). The physical examination can be therapeutic in confirming the child's sense of physical intactness and normality.

Genital and Perianal Examination

Once the general examination is complete, the examiner should make a smooth transition to the genital examination. Continued explanation to the child as to what is occurring helps ensure the child's continued cooperation as the examination proceeds.

Lighting and Privacy

An optimal examination of the genitalia requires proper lighting, privacy, adequate positioning, and cooperation. It is appropriate to drape the older child. The younger child may be more frightened by drapes and may actually want to see what is happening during the examination. A video colposcope allows the child to observe the genital and anal examination as it proceeds and helps demystify what the child is experiencing.

The emotional state of the child and the examiner's experience and intuition should guide the examination.

Positioning   A number of positions have been described for examination of the prepubertal child. This manual describes the supine frog-leg, the prone knee-chest, and the lateral decubitus positions. There are benefits to each; the examiner will need to decide whether one or a combination of positions is necessary. The supine frog-leg position offers the child relative comfort and provides the examiner with a clear view of the genitalia and anus. This position may be assumed in the lap of a parent or other ally or on the examination table.

The prone knee-chest position offers an excellent view of the anus and allows for another view of the hymenal membrane. In this position, the anterior wall of the vagina falls forward and allows the hymen to splay out for easy viewing. Efforts should be made to avoid a position that replicates the position in which the child was assaulted. For example, a child who was sodomized in a position similar to the knee-chest position may express signs of discomfort if placed in this position for the examination. In prepubertal children, both the frog-leg and knee-chest positions may be needed to examine the genital structures fully.

The examination is an exercise in looking, touching, and sampling (Cantwell, 1987). The examiner relies on inspection and gentle palpation to view all the necessary structures. The majority of examinations do not require instrumentation. If a colposcope is available to assist in the examination of the child, efforts should be made to demystify its use.

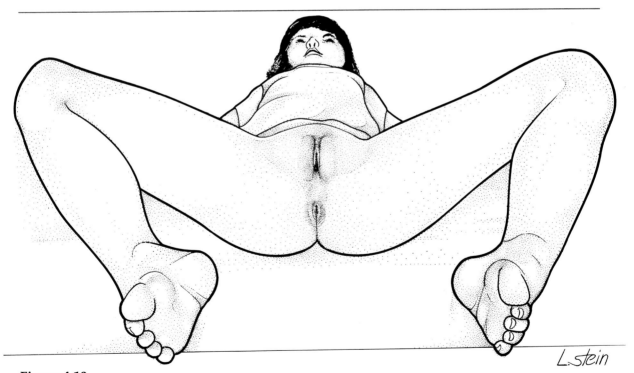

Figure 4.10
Supine Frog-Leg Position for Genital Examination

Figure 4.11
Supine Frog-Leg Position While in Mother's Lap

EVALUATION OF SEXUAL ABUSE IN THE PREPUBERTAL CHILD

Figure 4.12
Prone Knee-Chest Position for Genital Examination

**Examining
the External
and Internal
Structures**

An internal examination, such as a bimanual, speculum, or rectal examination, in prepubertal children is not routinely indicated, because it is unlikely to provide valuable forensic information. In the pubertal child, an internal examination is more appropriate if visual examination suggests that penile-vaginal penetration has occurred. A rectal examination is not routinely necessary; its only value is to assess sphincter tone and the presence of stool in the ampulla. Because external palpation and traction on the buttocks are generally sufficient to assess tone, a digital rectal examination is unnecessary in most cases. If a fissure or laceration of the external sphincter or anorectal canal is suspected, then the use of test tube proctoscopy or an anoscope is appropriate.

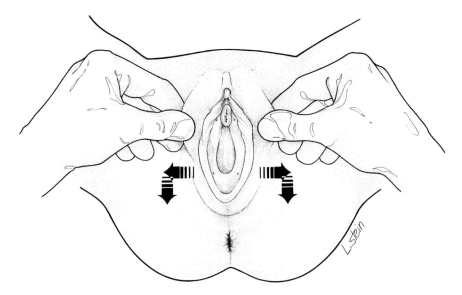

Figure 4.13
Technique for Examination of Female Genitalia in the Supine Frog-Leg
position

With the child in the frog-leg position, a downward outer traction on the labia majora will usually open the introitus for visual inspection (see Figure 4.13). If the child is in the prone knee-chest position, outward lateral pressure will accomplish the same (see Figure 4.15).

Vaginal Vestibule

The structures surrounding the vaginal vestibule are visually inspected first. Thus labial separation, traction, and changes in position may be utilized to observe all aspects of the tissues surrounding the vestibule.

Obvious acute injuries resulting in edema, abrasions, lacerations, puncture wounds, bruising, and bleeding should be noted. The examiner should also record information on the shape and contour of the hymen; the variability of the hymenal orifice diameter; any transections, distortions, redundancy, or signs of healed injury; and the appearance of the perihymenal tissues.

Size of
Hymenal Orifice

The size of the hymenal orifice is a controversial topic in the literature, and agreement as to its usefulness as a sole criterion for confirming sexual abuse has not been achieved. There is considerable variability in the transverse diameter of the hymenal orifice. The orifice diameter may vary considerably, depending upon the age of the child, the position in which the child is examined, the degree of relaxation, and the amount of traction on the labia utilized during the examination. The transverse diameter alone is rarely sufficient to determine whether a

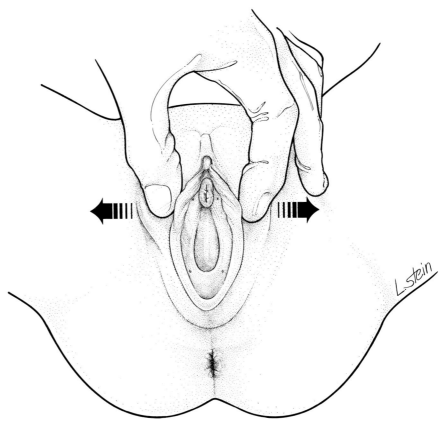

Figure 4.14
Alternate Technique for Examination in the Supine Frog-Leg Position

child has or has not been sexually abused and should not be used as a sole criterion for such a determination.

Anus and Perianal Area

The anus and perianal area are examined as well. Visually, the anal rugae are usually symmetric. Gentle traction or stroking of the perianal area should elicit reflex contraction of the sphincter muscle. Asymmetry of the rugal pattern, changes in pigmentation, discharge, signs of STDs, signs of trauma, and any laxity in the anal sphincter should be noted. Before interpreting that an abnormal response to traction is present, the examiner should be sure that the ampulla is free of stool, because the anus may naturally relax to evacuate such stool. Because controversy exists concerning the value of this finding alone, an abnormal response to traction without other signs of trauma should be interpreted cautiously. A wide, gaping anal opening and poor-to-absent reflex tightening with no stool in the ampulla is an abnormal finding.

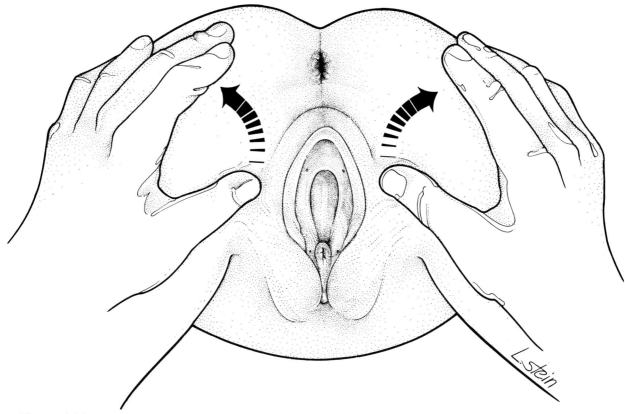

Figure 4.15
Technique for Examination of Female Genitalia in Prone Knee-Chest Position

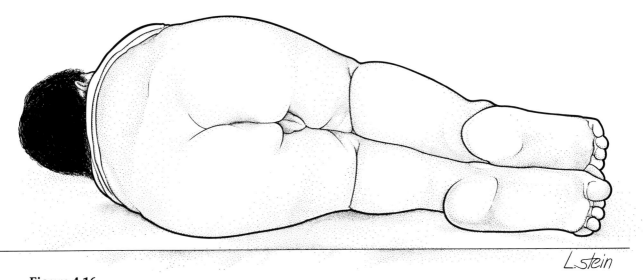

Figure 4.16
Position and Technique for Examination of Male Child in Left Lateral Decubitus (Cannonball) Position

EVALUATION OF SEXUAL ABUSE IN THE PREPUBERTAL CHILD

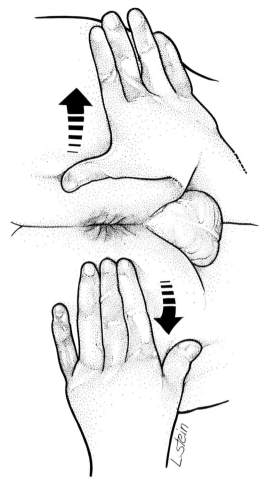

Figure 4.17
Technique for Examination of Male Child
in Left Lateral Decubitus Position

LABORATORY EVALUATION

**Collection
of Specimens**

Generally, the collection of specimens takes place along with the orderly examination of the child. The sequence of the examination suggests an obvious and timely manner of obtaining the required specimens (Finkel, 1988a). It is not necessary or appropriate to obtain every specimen discussed in this section for each case. The child's history and the physical examination will determine which specimens are necessary. However, because the examiner usually has only one opportunity to collect the specimens, it is better to err on the side of obtaining too many rather than too few.

Standard Studies   The following constitute a standard sexual abuse laboratory workup. Results for these studies should be obtained in most cases of suspected sexual abuse (see Chapter 6):

1. GC cultures of oropharynx, vagina/urethra, and rectum
2. Chlamydia *culture* of vagina/urethra and rectum
3. Serum for RPR
4. If vaginal/urethral/anal discharge present, collection of following specimens: specimen of discharge for Gram's stain; wet prep for trichomonas; specimen of discharge for culture of other STDs
5. Stool guaiac in cases of anal penetration by digits, foreign body, or penis
6. Urine pregnancy test in the postmenarcheal child

If sexual contact has occurred within 72 hours of the examination, use of a "rape kit" may be indicated, especially if the perpetrator is suspected of having ejaculated. The rape kit, although initially developed for adults, is a helpful tool in the evaluation of sexual abuse in children when evidence of the perpetrator's secretions or hair are likely to be found on the victim. A typical rape kit contains the following:

1. Victim consent forms
2. Specimen collection checklist
3. Brown paper (not plastic) bags for clothing
4. Tubes with swabs to collect secretions
5. Glass slides
6. Nonheparinized tubes for blood typing and syphilis serology
7. Orange sticks for fingernail scraping
8. Combs for collection of pubic and scalp hair
9. Envelopes for hair, nail scrapings
10. Gauze square or several swabs with tube for saliva sample
11. Tamper-proof seal
12. Routing form and information label for signatures of specimen handlers

Most emergency departments have rape kits to assist the examiner in the orderly collection of all the necessary specimens. The routine specimens, as well as the contents of the kit, constitute part of the forensic evidence. The laboratory findings may be helpful in corroborating inappropriate contact and in identifying the perpetrator. The absence of laboratory findings, however, does not disprove the child's history.

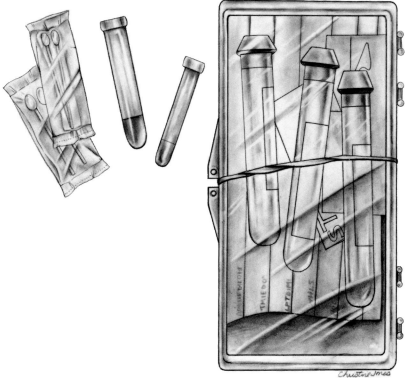

Figure 4.18
Typical Rape Kit

Forensic Evidence

Some general guidelines that are helpful for specimen collection are as follows:

1. Obtain the consent of victim or guardian.
2. Limit number of personnel involved in handling specimens.
3. Use standardized collection kits.
4. Use specific collection checklist.
5. Maintain chain of evidence.
6. Gloves should be worn to:
   a. Protect examiner from STDs
   b. Protect against contaminating the specimens with the examiner's blood-type secretions present in perspiration

The following detailed outline by De Jong (1988) is helpful in organizing the collection of forensic specimens necessary for the rape kit completed in the context of a sexual abuse evaluation. De Jong provides a clear explanation of some of the less familiar tests performed in this aspect of the evaluation, and gives the examiner some helpful advice concerning the collection of forensic evidence:

Description

I. Sperm.
    A. Motile sperm.
        1. Detected using a wet mount.
        2. May be present for only ½ hour and rarely seen after 6 to 8 hours. Shorter life span in oral cavity and longer life span in cervix.
    B. Nonmotile sperm.
        1. Detected on wet mount and/or Pap technique.
        2. May be present for up to 12-20 hours and rarely after 48-72 hours. Shorter duration in oral cavity.
        3. May be detected on clothing for up to 12 months.

II. Seminal fluid.
    A. Genetic markers.
        1. Approximately 80% of the population are "secretors," and all of their body fluids, including semen and saliva, will contain blood group antigens.
        2. Approximately 20% of the population are "nonsecretors," and their fluids can be identified by the presence of Lewis substance.
        3. Control samples are necessary from the victim, to identify his or her secretor status.
    B. Acid phosphatase.
        1. Acid phosphatase is a sensitive indicator of recent intercourse, owing to the relatively rapid decay of sperm. Acid phosphatase may be found in low levels in vaginal secretions, and a marked elevation in vaginal secretions correlates to intercourse within the preceding 24-48 hours. The acid phosphatase of prostatic origin is found in high concentration in semen.
        2. Elevations are of shorter duration in mouth and rectum.
        3. May persist on clothing in a dried state for months to years.
    C. P-30 semen glycoprotein of prostatic origin.
        1. Not found in vaginal fluid, urine, or saliva in females.
        2. Present in high levels in semen and in low levels in male urine. It is present in normal and vasectomized males.
        3. Positive P-30 means sexual contact has occurred within the last 48 hours. In dried state it may be detectable for up to 12 years.

III. Blood. Blood found on victim may be either the victim's or the perpetrator's, and samples of each will be necessary.

IV. Hair analysis. Direct microscopy of hair samples is much less specific than the fluid analyses above. The wide variability of hair types in the same individual, depending on site, allows the forensic pathologist only the ability to say that the sample provided is consistent with, inconsistent with, or inconclusive, when compared with hair from the alleged perpetrator.

V. Limitations.
    A. If ejaculation has not occurred, or if a condom is used, the tests for sperm, acid phosphatase, and P-30 will be negative.
    B. If perpetrator has aspermia or a vasectomy, tests for sperm will be negative, but acid phosphatase and P-30 will be positive.
    C. Of adult women studied within 24 hours of unprotected sexual intercourse, only 50-60% had sperm detected, and between 40-84% had acid phosphatase detected.

Collection of Specimens

I. Detection of sperm, semen, P-30, acid phosphatase, and blood group antigens. Obtain two to three swabbed specimens from each area of the body assaulted for sperm/semen analysis, P-30, and blood group antigens.
    A. Mouth: Swab under tongue and buccal pouch next to upper and lower molars. If patient gagged during ejaculation, obtain a swab of the nasopharynx.
    B. Vagina: Use dry or moistened swab, pass through vaginal opening and, if possible, leave in place for 1 minute or more. An alternative method is to instill 2 cc of sterile saline and then collect the wash using a medicine dropper or swab.
    C. Rectum: Insert swab at least ½ inch beyond anus.
    D. Take specimens from any suspicious areas on body surface.
        1. Dried semen or blood can be scraped with the back of a sterile scalpel blade and placed into a paper envelope found in the rape kit.
        2. Dried secretions that cannot be scraped can be lifted by utilizing a sterile cotton swab moistened with sterile water. Do not soak the swab, merely moisten it with a few drops of saline.
        3. Collect moist secretions with a sterile, dry cotton swab to avoid dilution.
        4. Collect two to three swabs from each area.
        5. Label all specimens.
        6. *Air dry* all specimens *for 60 minutes* for optimal preservation.
II. Detection of motile sperm. A wet mount should be utilized to identify the presence of motile sperm cells.
    A. Swab secretion to be examined and roll swab back and forth on slide with one drop of saline or special "hepes" media used for motile sperm examination.
    B. Place a cover slip on slide and allow swab to air dry.
    C. Examine slide immediately under 400x magnification and note presence or absence of sperm, and whether or not they are motile. This information may be helpful in determining time of assault.

D. After microscopic examination, fix the labeled slide with Pap smear fixative and stored it in cardboard mailer.

III. Fingernail scrapings, pubic hair, and foreign material.
   A. Place fingernail scrapings into paper envelopes using orange sticks.
   B. If pubertal development has begun, collect combed pubic hair into one envelope and 3-6 plucked pubic hairs from victim in another envelope. If the alleged perpetrator is known to the child, do not pull the child's hair unless the forensic laboratory indicates that the child's sample will be of use.
   C. Save and bag any foreign material found upon removal of the child's clothing.

IV. Victim's clothing. If the child has not changed clothing since the reported incident, it may be necessary to collect the clothes as evidence, because they may contain the pepetrator's secretions or other physical traces. Inspection of the clothes is helpful if the abuse involved more direct genital contact. If the abuse involved exposure or fondling only, collection of the clothes is not necessary. Clothing collection is most valuable in the acute setting. The child's clothing must be collected in a paper bag. The heat and humidity that can develop if clothing is placed in a plastic bag may denigrate the evidence. If the child has changed clothes or if the abuse occurred some time before the visit, efforts should be made to retrieve any articles of clothing that may have been contaminated with the perpetrator's secretions, even if the articles have been washed.

V. Victim identification.
   A. Secretor status of victim. Collect a saliva specimen from the victim by having the child place a sterile 2 × 2 gauze pad in his or her mouth; after it is sufficiently moistened with saliva, place it in a sterile tube.
   B. Blood type of victim. Collect blood sample from victim in appropriate tube for blood typing.

With the above information as background, the practitioner should be adequately prepared to collect the necessary laboratory specimens indicated in a specific case. The presence of specimen evidence is helpful in the documentation of the case. However, it must be reiterated that the absence of such evidence does not contradict the child's history of abuse.

In Brief
- The physical examination in the evaluation of sexual abuse allows for (a) discovery of residual findings from physical abuse and (b) reassurance of the child's intactness.

- Findings of sequelae or residua are not essential to the diagnosis of sexual abuse, and their absence does not negate the child's story.
- Conservative estimates place the probability of finding physical sequelae on the genital examination from sexually abusive behavior at about 25% (De Jong, 1988).
- The Huffman staging system describes estrogen effects in female children.
- The Tanner staging system describes pubertal changes in males and females as evidenced by genital and pubic hair development in males, and breast and pubic hair development in females.
- No absolute standards for the description of the hymen exist. The examiner does well to describe the overall condition of what is seen by describing the shape of the orifice and presence or absence of acute or chronic signs of injury.
- The two most common positions for the genital examination of the prepubertal child are the supine frog-leg and prone knee-chest positions.
- In addition to obtaining cultures for the most common STDs, rape kits are available for the collection of other forms of forensic evidence if indicated by the clinical situation.
- The terms *intact hymen* and *virginal hymen* are inexact and should not be used in conversation or in documentation of findings.
- The evaluation of the child should proceed in a head-to-toe sequence.

5 Differential Diagnosis of Anogenital Findings

This chapter outlines a differential diagnosis for signs and symptoms referable to the anogenital area. Discussion is presented of conditions whose physical findings may appear similar to those observed in sexual abuse and may potentially be confused with such. The evaluation of anogenital signs and symptoms such as erythema, excoriation, pruritus, bruising, bleeding, genital discharge, and unusual anogenital appearance can be especially problematic, and the differential diagnosis should always include sexual abuse. The health care practitioner must pay careful attention to the history given by the child and his or her caregivers, as well as to the physical and laboratory evaluations. In discussing the various etiologies for physical findings in the anogenital area, we in no way seek to diminish the need for consideration of sexual abuse.

The evaluation of cases of suspected sexual abuse is rarely straightforward. The presenting complaint in the child may include a variety of nonspecific behavioral changes. The physical examination frequently fails to uncover confirmatory findings of the alleged abuse. Physical findings, when present, are frequently nonspecific and not diagnostic on their own. The laboratory evaluation may be diagnostic only if seminal products or a sexually transmitted disease is identified. Differentiating conditions that appear similar to those found in cases of sexual abuse requires practice and experience. Consultation with the multidisciplinary team at a local or regional center may facilitate the health care professional's evaluation of the prepubertal child with anogenital complaints.

The signs and symptoms of vaginitis, vulvitis, and vulvovaginitis are commonly dealt with during the anogenital evaluation (Altchek, 1972). Vulvitis occurs when the structures constituting the vulva—labia majora, labia minora, clitoris, and components of the vestibule—are inflamed and friable. Vaginitis is diagnosed when the vaginal mucosa is inflamed, becomes friable and may bleed, and produces a discharge. Vulvovaginitis is diagnosed when both entities are present, one frequently leading to the other (Paradise, Campos, Friedman, & Frishmuth, 1982). Boys may also present with inflammation of the genitalia, but this occurs less frequently than in girls. In male children comparable inflammatory conditions affecting the most distal portion of the penis include phimosis, paraphimosis, and urethritis. Both male and female children may complain of perianal symptoms that result from inflammation due to infectious, dermatologic, and traumatic etiologies.

Framework for Consideration

Integral to considering a differential diagnosis and correctly interpreting anogenital findings is a careful history of the context in which the child's signs and symptoms were disclosed or became apparent to the caretakers. There are a number of conditions that may mimic some findings observed in children who have been sexually abused. It may be difficult to distinguish between these conditions and sexual abuse, especially for the clinician who only occasionally deals with anogenital complaints in the prepubertal child. A framework for consideration of the differential diagnosis of anogenital findings will help the primary care provider in progressing through an orderly consideration of the various diagnostic possibilities (Paradise, 1990).

Categorization and Etiologic Differential Diagnosis

Muram (1989) describes a classification system of anogenital findings that categorizes a variety of findings observed in prepubertal females. With slight modification, this system could be applied to the anogenital findings in males as well. The classification is as follows: Category 1 refers to genitalia with no abnormalities; Category 2 refers to nonspecific findings, including those findings related to sexual abuse as well as those due to other etiologies. These findings range from erythema to inflammation as a result of poor hygiene or as observed following inappropriate anogenital manipulation. Category 3 refers to findings strongly suggestive of sexual abuse, including lacerations to the hymen, vagina, and/or anus; bite marks to the external genitalia; and the presence of certain infections associated predominantly with sexual contact. Finally, Category 4 refers to definitive findings of sexual contact, namely, the presence of seminal products on the child. Clinically, definitive findings include those sexually transmitted diseases not contracted through vertical transmission.

Bays and Jenny (1990) describe conditions that might be confused with sexual abuse. They discuss the differential diagnosis of the range of conditions that could be found in Muram's (1989) nonspecific Category 3. These investigators break down the differential diagnosis of nonspecific anogenital conditions into a traditional etiologic categorization: (a) dermatologic, (b) congenital (anatomic/structural), (c) injuries, (d) infections, (e) anal, and (f) urethral. Tunnessen (1988) recommends a breakdown of the differential considerations as follows: (a) physiologic leukorrhea, (b) irritants, (c) infections, (d) systemic, (e) anatomic, and (f) miscellaneous. Finally, Emans and Goldstein (1990), in their authoritative text on pediatric gynecology, present a discussion of vulvovaginal problems in the prepubertal child encompassing the categories described and include recommendations for the treatment of the various conditions.

The following reflects our synthesis of the above categorizations in terms of the following signs and symptoms: (a) anogenital erythema, excoriation, and pruritus; (b) bruising in the anogenital area; (c) anogenital bleeding and/or bloody vaginal discharge; (d) nonbloody vaginal discharge; and (e) unusual anogenital appearance, both congenital and acquired.

Anogenital Erythema, Excoriation, Pruritus

Redness in the tissues of the genitalia and anus may result from a number of causes related to inflammation. Inflammation, irritation, and pruritus may lead to repeated scratching of the area and a worsening in the inflammatory process. A vicious cycle may ensue, with increased scratching and a continuation of the cycle. The causes of this situation could be local and/or systemic in origin. Whenever an inflammatory process is observed involving the genitalia or anus, inappropriate genital manipulation and STDs should be considered. Other possible causes to be considered, depending on the history and clinical index of suspicion, are local irritation, dermatologic disorders, infections, and, uncommonly, systemic conditions such as Crohn's disease, Kawasaki's syndrome, and Stevens-Johnson syndrome.

Local Irritation   Fecal contamination of the vagina from poor hygienic practices such as wiping the anogenital area from back to front (instead of the hygienic front to back) contributes to the development of vaginitis and its accompanying irritation and pruritus (Paradise et al., 1982). In obese children, retained urine in the skin folds, reflux, and poor drainage of urine into the vagina may lead to inflammation and irritation as well (Tunnessen, 1988). Any type of restrictive or poorly ventilated clothing, whether underwear, pants, or tights, may lead to friction and increased heat that can result in inflammation, irritation, pruritus, and erythema (Altchek, 1985). Additionally, chemical irritants such as soaps, fragrances, colored toilet tissue, and bubble baths may lead to inflammation in the anogenital area as well. Finally, sandbox vulvitis is caused by the entrapment of particles of dirt or sand in the child's vulvar area (Altchek, 1972; Tunnessen, 1988). In the prepubertal child, the labia majora do not fully surround the vulvar structures, and the child may come into contact with contaminating particulate material when sitting on the ground while at play outdoors.

Dermatologic   Atopic dermatitis is a relapsing skin condition characterized by intermittent inflammatory reactions superimposed on excessively dry and pruritic skin. Children with this condition frequently have personal or family histories of hay fever, asthma, and/or eczema. Signs of atopy frequently involve other sites of the body, with characteristic patterns (Gordon, 1983). Contact dermatitis is a skin irritation that results after contact with substances to which the skin is sensitive, typically on an allergic basis (Williams, Callen, & Owen, 1986). Seborrhea in the genital area is common in infancy, although it may occur at any age. It involves the folds of the diaper area between the labia minora and labia majora. Seborrheic rashes are pruritic and frequently become secondarily infected as a result of breaks to the protective barriers of the skin that arise from scratching. Seborrheic lesions in the genital area are elevated and erythematous. The yellow, greasy scales of seborrhea are also commonly observed in extragenital areas (Gordon, 1983; Williams et al., 1986). Psoriasis is a dermatologic condition that may affect the child at any age. The diagnostic lesions, although variable in size and location, are sharply demarcated, pruritic, erythematous plaques with silvery scales on a flat surface (Gordon, 1983).

Lichen sclerosus is an uncommon dermatologic condition of unknown etiology that typically presents in the anogenital area. In females, it presents as irregular ivory macules or papules that coalesce to form atrophic hypopigmented plaques in an hourglass or figure-eight pattern (Berth-Jones, Graham-Brown, & Burns, 1989; Loening-Baucke, 1991). In males, lichen sclerosus, known as balanitis xerotica obliterans, presents as a chronic,

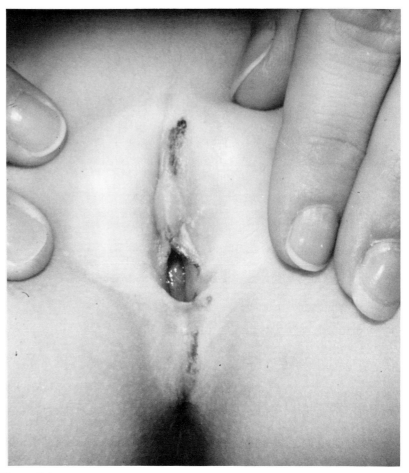

Photo 5.1
Lichen Sclerosus
A 2-year-old examined in supine frog-leg position with atrophic ivory-colored skin involving the labia majora and extending to perianal area. Skin is shiny, thin, and friable, and clearly demarcated from normal skin. Excoriation present above clitoral hood and on perineum. The hymen is spared. (Note: The examiner should wear gloves.) (Photograph courtesy of Dr. Cindy W. Christian, Philadelphia, PA)

progressive, atrophic, sclerosing process of the glans and foreskin (Laymon & Freeman, 1944; Rickwood, Hemalatha, Batcup, & Spitz, 1980). The skin in both the male and female becomes thin and fissured, may appear reddened and edematous, and is easily traumatized by minimal pressure.

Infections   Infection caused by STDs may lead to local irritation and redness (see Chapter 6 for a complete discussion). Nonspecific vaginitis is a mixed bacterial infection caused by a combination of coliforms, streptococci, *H. vaginalis*, and other bacteria (Emans, 1986). Vaginitis frequently leads to a secondary vulvitis with

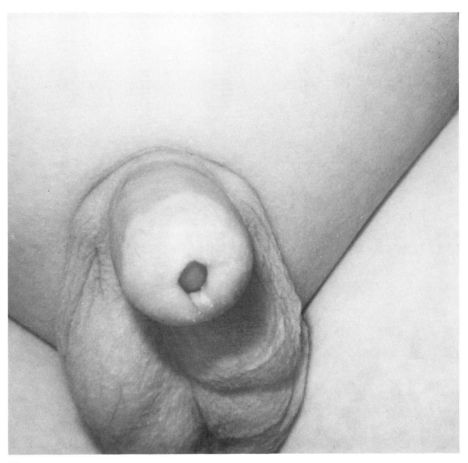

Photo 5.2
Balanitis Xerotica Obliterans
A 1-year-old photographed while sitting on examination table who developed sclerotic, atrophic, and hypopigmented foreskin that is not retractable over glans. Skin is thin and friable and has decreased elasticity. (Photograph courtesy of Drs. John W. Duckett and Howard M. Snyder, Philadelphia, PA)

local irritation, inflammation, erythema, and pruritus (Altchek, 1972). Infestation with pinworms is another cause of vulvovaginitis in prepubertal children. The female pinworm (*Enterobius vermicularis*) resides in the intestinal tract of the child and migrates to the anogenital area to deposit eggs. This causes pruritus, scratching, and irritation. Pinworms may move from the rectum to the vagina and can introduce fecal flora into the vagina, resulting in a bacterial vulvovaginitis (Altchek, 1972).

Scabies, found in cases of close physical contact (Gordon, 1983), is caused by a parasitic mite (*Sarcoptes scabiei*) and results in the development of pruritic erythematous papules with wavy burrows.

Candidal overgrowth of the genital tract is unusual in the prepubertal child. It may occur in the following situations: (a)

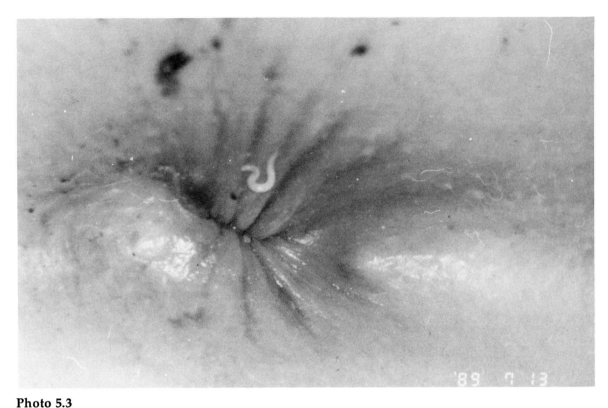

Photo 5.3
Pinworm
*A 4-year-old male examined in left lateral decubitus position with perianal excoriation secondary to pruritus from pinworms (*Enterobius vermicularis*).*

after a course of antibiotics, (b) with diabetes mellitus, (c) when the child is in diapers, or (d) as a result of other risk factors, namely, immunodeficiency (Emans & Goldstein, 1990). Antibiotics change the makeup of the vaginal flora that typically serve to keep the yeast in check.

Finally, perianal streptococcal cellulitis is recognized as an etiology leading to a perianal rash that has an intense confluent area of erythema surrounding the anus (Spear, Rothbaum, Keating, Blaufuss, & Rosenblum, 1985). The rash is described as being irregular, but well demarcated. The condition may cause painful defecation, blood-streaked stools, and perianal inflammation and irritation. The relationship of perianal streptococcal cellulitis to group A beta-hemolytic streptococcal vulvovaginitis has not been fully identified.

Systemic

Inflammatory bowel disease, or Crohn's disease, may cause vulvar or perianal involvement. Several reports exist of cases in which these findings have been confused with sexual abuse (Clayden, 1987; Hobbs & Wynne, 1987).

TABLE 5.1 Differential Diagnosis of Anogenital Erythema, Excoriation, and Pruritus

Local Irritation	Dermatologic	Infection	Systemic
Sexual abuse	Atopic dermatitis	Sexually transmitted disease	Crohn's disease
Poor hygiene	Contact dermatitis	Nonspecific vaginitis	Kawasaki's syndrome
Tight/poorly ventilated underwear	Seborrheic dermatitis	Pinworms	Stevens-Johnson syndrome
Chemical	Diaper dermatitis/ candida	Scabies	
Sandbox vaginitis	Psoriasis	Candidal	
	Lichen sclerosus/ balanitis xerotica obliterans	Perianal strepto-coccal cellulitis	

Kawasaki syndrome has cutaneous manifestations as one of its diagnostic criteria. The skin findings may involve the anogenital area; one report describes two patients with a perineal rash that was erythematous and macular, became confluent, and eventually desquamated (Fink, 1983). The rash appeared to be painful and pruritic. Although not confused with sexual abuse, this case suggests that Kawasaki's syndrome be included in the differential of anogenital inflammation.

Stevens-Johnson syndrome, with its characteristic mucositis, may lead to vulvovaginitis and should be considered in its differential (Emans, 1986).

Anogenital Bruising

The differential diagnosis of anogenital trauma manifested by genital or anal bruising includes both sexual abuse and nonsexually sustained blunt and impaling injuries. An appropriate and plausible history should accompany the history of any injury. Bruising in the genital area may also be seen in a variety of hematologic, connective tissue, and dermatologic conditions (Bays & Jenny, 1990).

Local Injury

The most common nonsexual injury to the genitalia is the straddle injury. This occurs when the child falls upon a hard object, crushing the soft tissues between the object and pubic bone. Such injuries tend to be unilateral and anterior. The hymen, an internal structure, is not affected by this mechanism of injury. Impaling or penetrating injuries, however, such as a fall onto an exposed nail, a stick, or broom handle, may injure the hymen or anus. Other types of trauma, including motor vehicle accidents,

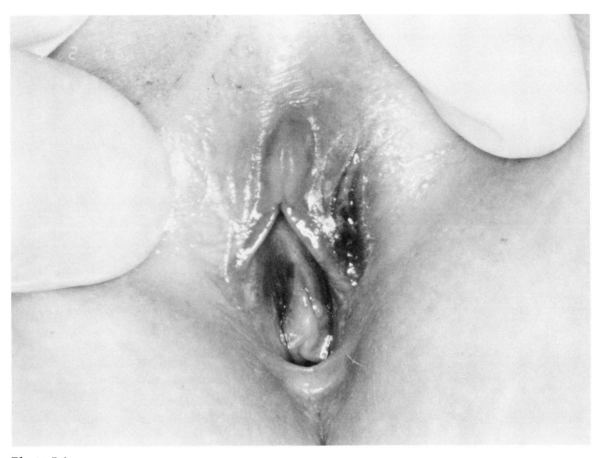

Photo 5.4
Straddle Injury
A 6-year-old examined in the supine frog-leg position demonstrating a crush laceration, with fresh bleeding and tissue edema between left labia majora and clitoral hood. Injury occurred during a fall onto a bicycle crossbar. Injury did not involve the hymen.

may also cause injury to the anogenital area (Baker, 1986). Male children may incur genital trauma if an object such as a toilet seat falls upon the penis. In addition, zipper injuries to the penis may be seen.

Dermatologic

In infants and toddlers, Mongolian spots, which are slate blue, well-demarcated areas of hyperpigmentation, may be confused with bruising. Mongolian spots are found in more than one-half of the black population and occasionally in white children (Behrman & Kliegman, 1983). They are usually on the back and buttocks.

Lichen sclerosus is prone to local trauma from minimal pressure and may become blue and discolored as a result. Vascular nevi may give the appearance of bruising secondary to the visible accentuation of the capillary bed underneath the skin.

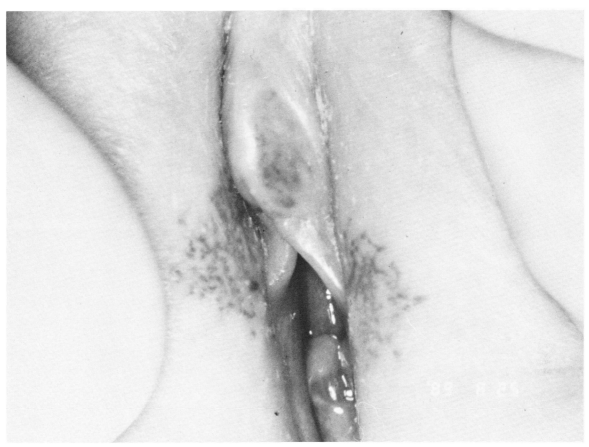

Photo 5.5
Vascular Nevus
A 5-year-old examined in the supine frog-leg position with a vascular nevus that blanches with pressure. It involves the clitoral hood, the medial aspect of the labia majora, and the lateral aspects of the labia minora.

Phytodermatitis mimics bruising and burns on the child's skin and has been confused with child physical abuse (Coffman, Boyce, & Hansen, 1985; Dannaker, Glover, & Goltz, 1988). This condition occurs when the child's skin comes in contact with plant psorlens (e.g., lemon juice) and then is exposed to sunlight, leaving a discoloration. If this is offered as a reason for anogenital bruising, the history must account for contact with the psorlen and exposure of the anogenital skin to sunlight.

Systemic   Bleeding disorders such as hemophilia, Von Willebrand's disease, and idiopathic thrombocytopenic purpura (ITP) may all lead to anogenital bruising. Bruising in extragenital sites is typical, however, and appropriate laboratory studies should rule these possibilities in or out. In addition, disorders with vasculitis as a component may cause bruising in the anogenital area.

TABLE 5.2 Anogenital Bruising

Local Injury	Dermatologic	Systemic
Straddle injury	Mongolian spots	Bleeding disorder
Impaling injury	Lichen sclerosus/balanitis	Vasculitis
(nail, broom handle)	xerotica obliterans	
Motor vehicle trauma	Vascular nevi	
	Phytodermatitis	

Anogenital Bleeding and/or Bloody Vaginal Discharge

Bleeding localized to the anogenital area may represent a medical emergency, and requires identification of the source of the bleeding and its etiology. Bloody or blood-tinged vaginal or urethral discharge is a separate clinical entity that may initially be difficult to differentiate from anogenital bleeding. The bloody discharge, like frank bleeding, requires diagnosis and treatment.

Local Irritation

Bleeding may arise in the anogenital region as a result of inappropriate anogenital manipulation from sexual abuse. Although nonaccidental trauma should always be considered to be due to sexual abuse, the differential diagnosis of localized injury and bleeding includes accidental trauma, superficial abrasions, and friability of the mucosa from a vulvovaginitis. A foul-smelling vaginal discharge raises the possibility of a foreign body. When a foreign body is present, the discharge may be bloody (Paradise & Willis, 1985). Toilet tissue is the most frequently described such foreign body.

Dermatologic

Bleeding may also result from the effects of pruritic dermatologic conditions such as atopic, contact, and seborrheic dermatitis as well as from psoriasis and lichen sclerosus. The inflammation leads to pruritus and irritation and ultimately to local trauma and bleeding.

Infection

Infections can cause the vaginal and vulvar tissues to become friable and to bleed. STDs contracted during sexual abuse have characteristic discharges and may lead to a vulvovaginitis (see Chapter 6). Some less common genital infections may do this as well. Group A beta-hemolytic streptococcus may cause a vaginitis, especially following a pharyngitis (Altchek, 1985). *Shigella* and *Yersinia* cause similar findings and should be considered if diarrhea is part of the presentation (Emans & Goldstein, 1990; Murphy & Nelson, 1979; Watkins & Quan, 1984).

Endocrinologic

Bleeding from the vagina may be menstrual flow from precocious pubertal development. Hormone-producing tumors should

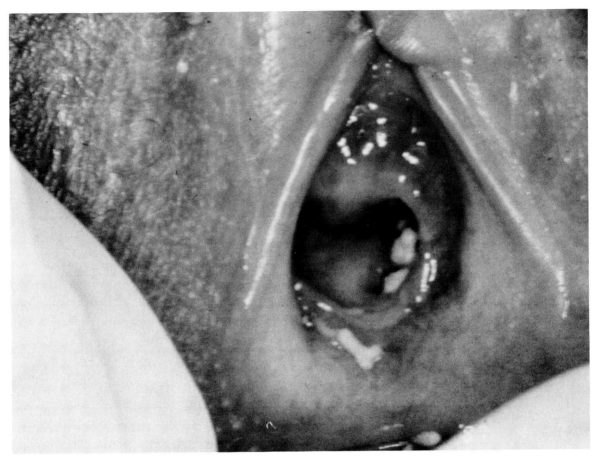

Photo 5.6
Foreign Body
An 8-year-old examined in the supine frog-leg position with crescentic hymenal orifice and a narrow posterior rim. Patient complains of chronic vaginal discharge. Discharge present on examination, with foul odor, erythema, and friability of tissues of the vaginal wall secondary to foreign body of tissue paper.

be excluded, and endocrinologic evaluation will be necessary (Breen & Maxson, 1977). When an endocrinologic reason for bleeding is present, signs of genital trauma will be absent. In addition, in the female neonate, a bloody discharge may be transiently observed during the first weeks of life as a result of maternal estrogen withdrawal.

Structural/Neoplastic   Vaginal polyps are benign growths that may erode and bleed. A vulvar hemangioma may ulcerate and bleed as well (Levin & Selbst, 1988). Finally, sarcoma botryoides, a grapelike malignant tumor that typically arises from the anterior vaginal wall near the cervix and may involve the vagina, uterus, bladder, and urethra, may present as vaginal bleeding (Emans & Goldstein, 1990). Its peak incidence is in the first two years of life, with most cases presenting before 5 years of age. Prognosis is poor unless found early, so all suspicious lesions should be fully evaluated.

TABLE 5.3 Anogenital Bleeding and/or Bloody Vaginal Discharge

Local Irritation	Dermatologic	Infection	Endocrine	Miscellaneous
Nonaccidental trauma/ sexual abuse Accidental trauma Foreign body	Lichen sclerosus Atopic dermatitis Contact dermatitis Seborrheic dermatitis	STDs Vulvo/ vaginitis Group A strep Shigella Yersinia	Estrogen withdrawal (neonate) Precocious puberty from hormone-producing tumors/ idiopathic	Vaginal polyp Vulvar hemangioma Sarcoma botryoides

Nonbloody Vaginal Discharge

Vaginal discharge is a common anogenital complaint that requires evaluation. Leukorrhea, a physiologic clear white, mucoid discharge, is a normal variant in the prepubertal child and should not be confused with the pathologic discharges associated with any of the causes of vulvitis, vaginitis, and vulvovaginitis already discussed (Emans & Goldstein, 1990). A host of infections are associated with vaginal discharges, and STDs as well as some nonsexually acquired infections frequently have associated discharges (see Chapter 6). Additionally, a number of systemic infections are associated with discharges, including varicella, measles, scarlet fever, and typhoid.

Congenital anomalies of the genitourinary tract may contribute to persistent wetness and be initially misdiagnosed as a discharge or they may lead to inflammation in the anogenital

TABLE 5.4 Nonbloody Vaginal Discharge

Local Irritation	Infection	Systemic	Anatomic
Sexual abuse Foreign body Chemical irritant Restrictive clothing	STDs Nonspecific vaginitis/ coliforms Diphtheria Group A strep H. influenza Mycoplasma N. menigitidis S. aureus Secondary infection from scratching Shigella S. pneumonia Yersinia	Physiologic/ leukorrhea Infections: measles, scarlet fever, typhoid, varicella	Ectopic ureter Rectovaginal fistula Pelvic abscess

area, causing a vulvovaginitis. An ectopic ureter may drain into the vagina, cervix, uterus, or urethra. It may cause minimal daytime wetness but can produce purulent perineal discharge, especially if a kidney infection is present (Emans & Goldstein, 1990). A rectovaginal fistula may also lead to similar findings. Finally, an acquired draining pelvic abscess could lead to similar findings as well.

Unusual Anatomic Appearance

The health care provider may be called upon to evaluate the appearance of various genital structures and determine if they are normal in appearance. Both congenital and acquired anomalies of the genitourinary tract may alter the expected appearance of the genital structures. These findings may simulate the chronic changes observed in anogenital appearance after sexual abuse.

Acquired

Abnormalities in anogenital appearance may arise from such acquired conditions as labial agglutination, urethral prolapse, labial abscess, paraphimosis, phimosis, and hair-thread tourniquet syndrome. The acquired conditions may arise from both sexual and nonsexual etiologies.

Labial agglutination (or labial adhesions) occurs when the labia minora join in the midline as a result of inflamed surfaces adhering and then fusing. This fusion may be near total and may cause poor drainage of vaginal secretions and diversion of urinary flow. Labial adhesions are believed to be secondary to vulvar irritation and poor hygiene. Labial adhesions are believed to be acquired typically in a nonsexual fashion; however, genital fondling or vulvar coitus may result in irritation of the medial aspects of the labia minora and predispose to agglutination (Berkowitz, Elvik, & Logan, 1987a; McCann, Voris, & Simon, 1988).

Urethral prolapse occurs when the distal portion of the female urethral mucosa becomes everted and edematous, creating the appearance of a doughnut-shaped structure surrounding the urethral meatus (Johnson, 1991; Lowe, Hill, Jeffs, & Brendler, 1986). It is most common in prepubescent black girls and in many cases appears to be related to an antecedent episode of increased intra-abdominal pressure.

Phimosis and paraphimosis are conditions affecting the foreskin. Phimosis is a congenital or acquired inflammatory condition of the foreskin resulting in pathologic nonretractability that is not consistent with the developmentally normal state of nonretractability seen in most young boys (Rickwood et al., 1980). If left untreated, phimosis results in inadequate hygiene, severe

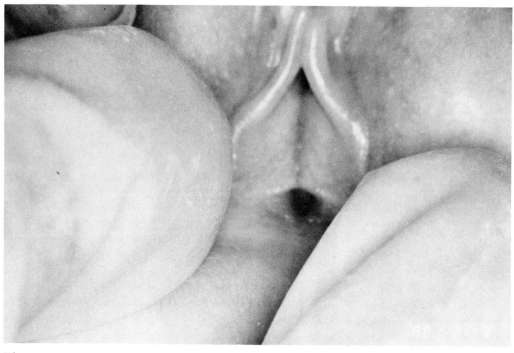

Photo 5.7
Labial Agglutination
A 3¹⁄₁₂-year-old examined in supine frog-leg position. Labia minora fused in midline with superior and inferior opening. Hymenal membrane not visualized due to agglutination.

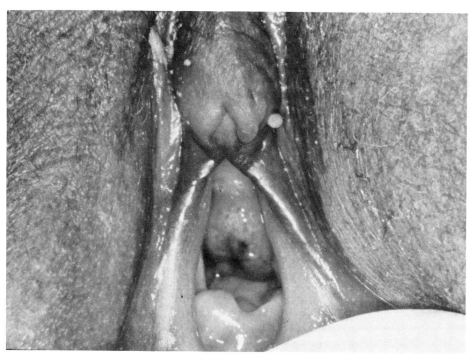

Photo 5.8
Urethral Prolapse
A 6-year-old examined in supine frog-leg position demonstrating eversion of urethral mucosa and prolapse through meatus with accompanying edema, and hemorrhage into periurethral tissues.

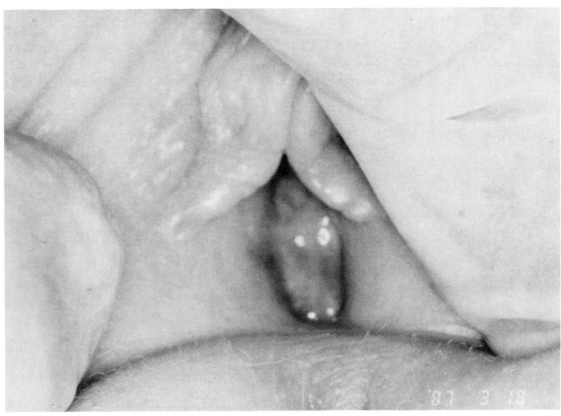

Photo 5.9
Imperforate Hymen
A 2¹¹⁄₁₂-year-old examined in supine frog-leg position with no hymenal orifice identifiable. Normal anatomic structures posterior following abdominal and pelvic ultrasound examination.

inflammation, and ulceration of the glans and undersurface of the prepuce (Dodson, 1970). Paraphimosis, on the other hand, is an acquired inflammatory condition that results when a retracted foreskin is left in the retracted position, causing venous and lymphatic obstruction. The distal penis becomes swollen and inflamed.

Finally, the hair-thread tourniquet syndrome may involve the genitalia. In this situation, fibers of hair or thread become tightly wrapped around external genitalia structures such as the penis, labia minora, and clitoris (Barton, Sloan, Nichter, & Reinisch, 1988; Press, Schachner, & Paul, 1980; Singh, Kim, & Wax, 1978). This tourniquet effect leads to varying degrees of lymphatic, venous, and arterial obstruction, with subsequent swelling, discoloration, ischemia, and eventually necrosis. Both accidental and intentional cases have been described (Barton et al., 1988).

Congenital   Congenital abnormalities such as imperforate hymen, vaginal septum, distal vaginal agenesis, phimosis, and ambiguous

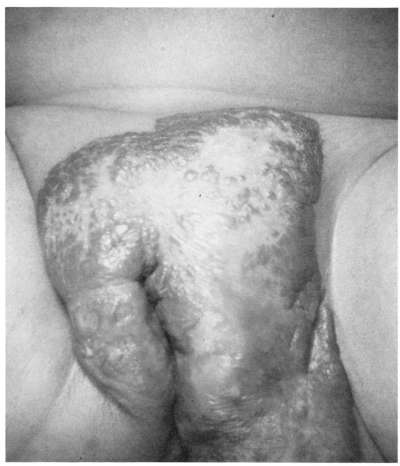

Photo 5.10
Vulvar Hemangioma
A 9-month-old with large hemangioma distorting mons pubis, labia majora, and extending into perineum. The vulvar hemangioma is demonstrating signs of initial involution most apparent over the mons pubis. (Photograph courtesy of Dr. Cindy W. Christian, Philadelphia, PA.)

genitalia may be present and may alter normal landmarks. Imperforate hymen is a congenital condition in which no hymenal orifice is present. If left untreated, mucocolpos (retention of vaginal secretions) may develop, and eventually hematocolpos (retention of menstrual flow) will develop at puberty with the onset of menses.

Other congenital anomalies that may alter the appearance of the genitalia include paraurethral cysts, urethral diverticulum, ectopic ureterocele, hymenal or vaginal cysts, vulvar hemangioma, congenital pit, and congenital failure of midline genital fusion (Adams & Horton, 1989; Bays & Jenny, 1990; Emans & Goldstein, 1990; Levin & Selbst, 1988).

TABLE 5.5   Unusual Anogenital Appearance

Acquired	Congenital
Labial agglutination	Imperforate hymen
Urethral prolapse	Hymenal or vaginal cysts
Phimosis	Phimosis
Paraphimosis	Vulvar hemangioma
Labial abscess	Congenital pit
Hair-thread tourniquet syndrome	Congenital failure of midline genital fusion
	Paraurethral cysts
	Urethral diverticulum
	Ectopic ureterocele

6 Sexually Transmitted Diseases

Sexually transmitted diseases are uncommonly found in prepubertal children (White, Loda, Ingram, & Pearson, 1983). The incidence of STDs increases markedly with the entrance of the child into the adolescent period, due to an increase in sexual activity within this age group.

Both the Centers for Disease Control (CDC) (1989) and the American Academy of Pediatrics (AAP, Committee on Early Childhood, 1983) have stated that any child with an STD must be suspected of being a victim of sexual abuse (see also White et al., 1983). Children with STDs must be presumed to have had contact with infected genital secretions in the context of sexually abusive behavior. Little support exists to justify the common belief that sexually transmitted diseases may be transmitted nonsexually by way of contact with inanimate objects (Neinstein, Goldenring, & Carpenter, 1984). Therefore, most children with STDs have acquired them through abusive sexual contact. Table 6.1 categorizes various STDs based on their usual mode of infection in the prepubertal child.

The child who presents with vulvovaginitis, vaginal discharge, dysuria, perianal irritation, or genital warts should be considered as a possible case of sexual victimization. Clearly, any child who presents for evaluation of suspected sexual abuse should be considered to have been exposed to STDs and needs appropriate testing as well. The sexually abused child is at risk

TABLE 6.1 Modes of STD Transmission: Probability of Being Caused by Sexual Abuse

Certain	Probable	Possible
Gonorrhea[a]	Chlamydia[a]	Herpes I (in genital area)
Syphilis[a]	Condyloma acuminata[a]	
	Trichomonas vaginalis	
	Herpes II	

SOURCE: AAP Committee on Child Abuse and Neglect (1991, p. 257). Reproduced by permission of *Pediatrics*, Vol. 87, p. 254. Copyright 1991.
a. If not perinatally acquired.

for contracting gonorrhea, chlamydia, and syphilis. As such, the history and physical examination findings should be evaluated for these infections. Other STDs have been described in sexual abuse victims, and the possibility of these should be considered by the investigator as well. Among these are herpes simplex, condyloma acuminata, trichomoniasis, HIV infection, and pediculosis pubis.

The Centers for Disease Control (1989) recommends that the following procedures and tests be performed at the initial evaluation of any prepubertal child suspected of being a victim of sexual abuse:

1. Gram stain of any genital or anal discharge
2. Culture of vagina/urethra, rectum, and pharynx for *N. gonorrhoeae*
3. Culture of vagina/urethra, rectum, and pharynx for *C. trachomatis*
4. Wet prep of vaginal secretions for *T. vaginalis*
5. Culture lesions for HSV
6. Serologic test for syphilis
7. Serologic test for HIV (based on the prevalence of the infection and on suspected risk)
8. Frozen serum sample

According to the CDC, the syphilis and HIV serology should be repeated in 12 weeks, and all other cultures should be repeated 10-14 days after initial examination in cases of acute assault.

Gonorrhea

Organism. Neisseria gonorrhoeae is a gram-negative diplococcus that has been extensively studied in the prepubertal child. It may be symptomatic or asymptomatic in presentation. Children with gonorrhea vaginitis or urethritis may present with purulent vaginal or urethral discharge for as long as eight weeks (White et al., 1983). Carriage of the organism has been reported

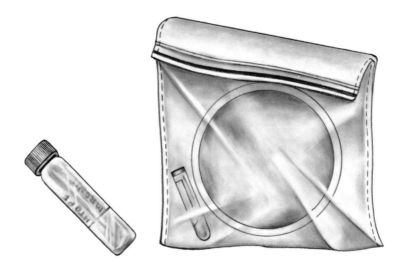

Figure 6.1
Glass tube with chlamydia culture media and GC plate in bag with high CO_2 environment.

for as long as six months without treatment, and pharyngeal and rectal infection are typically asymptomatic at presentation (White et al., 1983).

Transmission. Although the organism has been shown to survive for hours on inanimate objects, the literature has failed to document adequately such transmission to a child. One case is reported of a hospitalized soldier in 1939 who was suspected of contracting gonococcal urethritis after sharing a urinal with an infected soldier (Neinstein et al., 1984). The bulk of the evidence confirms that outside of the neonatal period, where vertical transmission occurs, gonorrhea in children, as in adults, is a sexually transmitted disease.

Identification. A Gram stain of genital or anal discharge is helpful but not diagnostic of the disease. A culture on Thayer-Martin media and one on chocolate agar incubated in high carbon dioxide environment are necessary for diagnosis. Besides high carbon dioxide environment, the plates need to be at room temperature, as cold plates may kill the organism on contact (Murphy, 1983). The examiner should keep in mind that *N. gonorrhoeae* are fastidious organisms. In addition, cotton-tipped applicators may be toxic, so only rayon-tipped swabs should be used (Horowitz, 1987). Rapid tests such as Gonozyme should not be utilized because of interference by other nonpathogenic *Neisseria* species. The microbiology lab utilized should report out specifically that *N. gonorrhoeae* has been isolated to avoid any confusion with other *Neisseria* species.

Treatment. Primary therapy when *sensitivity* is *unknown* or *penicillin resistant* is as follows:

1. For children less than 45 kilograms:
   ceftriaxone 125 mg IM × one dose
2. For children 45 kilograms or greater:
   ceftriaxone 250 mg IM × one dose

Primary therapy when the organism is *penicillin sensitive* is as follows:

1. For children less than 45 kilograms:
   amoxicillin 50 mg/kg po × one dose, plus
   probenecid 25 mg/kg po × one dose (max of 1 gm)
2. For children 45 kilograms or greater:
   amoxicillin 3 gm po × one dose, plus
   probenecid 1 gm po × one dose

The following therapy is appropriate if the patient is *penicillin allergic*:

Spectinomycin 40 mg/kilo IM × one dose (max of 2 gm)

Erythromycin, tetracycline, and doxycycline are not considered adequate therapy.

Chlamydia Trachomatis

Organism. Chlamydia trachomatis is an intracellular pathogen that may or may not be associated with symptoms. It is not believed to be a common cause of vulvovaginitis in the prepubertal female or in nongonococcal urethritis in prepubertal males. However, in the context of sexual abuse, this pathogen should be considered because of its high prevalence in the sexually active adult population. Any discharge from the vagina or urethra should be evaluated, especially if penicillin therapy fails.

Transmission. The bulk of evidence confirms sexual transmission. No definitive nonsexual transmission outside of the neonatal period has been reported (Neinstein et al., 1984).

Identification. Culture in special *Chlamydia* media is required. Rapid slides have been developed, and their sensitivity varies with the examiner's technique and the reporting laboratory. Most of the rapid tests are designed for the identification of

Chlamydia from cervical specimens obtained during a pelvic examination, and their use in the examination of a prepubertal child's vagina or anus is inappropriate. Rapid tests such as Chlamydiazyme or Microtrak *should not be used*. The *Chlamydia* culture, although a relatively expensive and lengthy test, remains the superior means of identifying infection in the prepubertal child.

Treatment. Erythromycin treatment is as follows:

1. For children less than 45 kilograms:
   erythromycin base or stearate 50 mg/kg po QID × 7 days
   erythromycin ethylsuccinate 70 mg/kg po QID × 7 days
2. For children 45 kilograms or greater:
   erythromycin base or stearate 500 mg po QID × 7 days
   erythromycin ethylsuccinate 800 mg po QID × 7 days

If the child is 8 years or older, recommended tetracycline or doxycycline treatment is as follows:

1. for children less than 45 kilograms:
   tetracycline 40 mg/kg po divided QID × 7 days
2. for children 45 kilograms or greater:
   tetracycline 500 mg po QID × 7 days, or doxycycline 100 mg po BID × 7 days

---

Syphilis

Organism. Syphilis is caused by *Treponema pallidum*, a spirochete responsible for the disease's widely varying presentation. At least four stages or phases have been described: congenital, primary, secondary, and tertiary or neurosyphilis. Pediatricians have historically been most concerned with the presentation and diagnosis of congenital syphilis that occurs through vertical transmission prenatally from infected mother to child. Any child outside of the neonatal period who presents with signs of syphilis that is confirmed by serologic testing must be evaluated for the possibility of sexual abuse.

Transmission. Sexual transmission is the predominant mode of transmission. Endemic treponemal diseases such as pinta and yaws may be transmitted by direct skin-to-skin contact. *T. pallidum*, which causes syphilis, is morphologically similar. Theoretically, this type of transmission could occur (Neinstein et al., 1984). However, the only reported cases of nonsexual transmission outside of the neonatal period have occurred through repeated contact with a primary chancre, and the child's subsequent findings have typically been in extragenital sites as well (Neinstein et al., 1984).

Identification. Identification of the *T. pallidum* spirochete in the primary or secondary lesion is at best difficult and requires skill and the availability of dark-field microscopy. In light of this, serologic testing is the most expeditious means of determining infection (Murphy, 1983). A serologic specimen for an RPR or VDRL should be obtained at the initial visit and then six weeks later.

Treatment. Penicillin treatment is as follows:

1. For primary, secondary, and latent of not more than one year's duration:
   benzathine penicillin G 50,000 units/kg IM × one dose (max of 2.4 million units)
2. For latent of greater than one year's duration:
   benzathine penicillin G 50,000 units/kg IM q wk × three doses
   (If clinically indicated, CSF examination should be performed and treatment guidelines for neurosyphilis in the CDC's *Morbidity and Mortality Weekly Reports* and the AAP's *Red Book* should be followed for positive findings and follow-up.)

For penicillin-allergic children with primary, secondary, and latent of not more than one year's duration, erythromycin treatment is as follows:

1. For children less than 45 kilograms:
   erythromycin base or stearate 50 mg/kg po QID × 2 weeks
   erythromycin ethylsuccinate 70 mg/kg po QID × 2 weeks
2. For children 45 kilograms or greater:
   erythromycin base or stearate 500 mg/kg po QID × 2 weeks
   erythromycin ethylsuccinate 800 mg/kg po QID × 2 weeks

Tetracycline or doxycycline treatment, for children 8 years or older, is as follows:

1. For children less than 45 kilograms:
   tetracycline 40 mg/kg po divided QID × 2 weeks
2. For children 45 kilograms or greater:
   tetracycline 500 mg po QID × 2 weeks

For penicillin-allergic children with latent of more than one year's duration but without CNS involvement, increase the above recommendations to 4 weeks' duration.

Condyloma Acuminata

Organism. Condyloma acuminata is caused by the human *papilloma* virus, a relative of the common skin wart virus, which prefers moist skin areas, such as the anogenital region. Presentation usually involves wartlike growths on the vulva or perianal area (De Jong et al., 1982). These warts must be differentiated from condyloma lata and rare perianal tumors. Typically, condyloma acuminata begin as small pinpoint papules that rapidly enlarge to form soft cauliflowerlike fibroepitheliomas. This is opposed to condyloma lata, which typically are flattened, broad-based lesions with relatively less surface area. Biopsy with typing of the lesions and serologic testing for the presence of syphilis will remove any uncertainty.

Transmission. Contact with lesions will spread the disease. Incubation period may be anywhere from 6 weeks to 20 months (White et al., 1983). Cases of vertical transmission from infected mother to child have been reported, as have cases of nonsexual transmission between caretakers and children secondary to close physical contact of a nonsexual nature. Although the possibility of sexual abuse should be considered in a child presenting with condyloma, it is not the only possibility that needs to be explored (Neinstein et al., 1984).

Identification. The characteristic appearance of the condyloma is usually sufficient to diagnose the lesions. At times, the lesions will not be classic, and biopsy and serologic testing will be helpful. Recently, tests have been developed that make the typing of lesions easier. Such tests will help in surveillance for risk of cervical cancer in those patients with the types most associated with cervical cancer (Merz, 1988).

Treatment. A number of treatment options exist, and the specific choice depends on the age of the child, extent of involvement, and stage of presentation. The skills of a pediatric dermatologist should be obtained to ensure appropriate treatment and adequate follow-up. Depending on the serotype and areas of involvement, the patient may require Pap smears on a routine basis.

1. Topical treatment consists of podophyllin 10%-25% applied topically, followed by thorough bathing 1-4 hours later q. wk × 4 weeks.
2. If lesions are extensive or difficult to treat, owing to their location, cryotherapy or laser surgery may be indicated.

Trichomoniasis

Organism. Trichomoniasis is caused by *Trichomonas vaginalis*, a single-celled flagellate protozoan whose normal habitat is the human vagina, urethra, bladder, Skene's and Bartholin's glands, prostate, anus, and, rarely, the foreskin (White et al., 1983). There are no animal vectors known. *T. vaginalis* is considered an uncommon infection in prepubertal children (Neinstein et al., 1984). In the sexually active adult population, however, it is a common cause of vaginitis and discharge. Typically, *T. vaginalis* is asymptomatic in the male carrier (White et al., 1983).

Transmission. The protozoan may survive in fresh water for up to 30 minutes and for up to two to three days in warm mineral water (Neinstein et al., 1984). It may also survive for several hours in urine. Speculation exists concerning the possibility that *T. vaginalis* may be transmitted by fomites in crowded, unhygienic situations. While there is a possibility that a shared warm, wet washcloth could be an infectious fomite, it is highly unlikely that a toilet seat or public swimming pool could be a common vector (Neinstein et al., 1984).

Vertical transmission from an infected mother to child at birth has been described, as has transmission from improperly cleaned medical instruments. Although *T. vaginalis* may at times be transmitted in a nonsexual manner, the possibility of sexual transmission to a prepubertal child must always be considered and disproved.

Identification. A saline wet prep is the ideal way to identify the protozoa. A swab of vaginal fluid is placed in 1 cc of saline, and a drop of this suspension is then placed on a slide. A cover slip is then applied and the slide is examined within 10 minutes of collection under high and low power.

Treatment. Metronidazole treatment consists of the following:

1. For children less than 45 kilograms:
   metronidazole 5 mg/kilo po TID × 7 days
2. For children 45 kilograms or greater:
   metronidazole 500 mg po BID × 7 days
3. For adolescents:
   metronidazole 2 gm po as a single dose

Herpes Genitalis

Organism. Genital herpes is caused by the DNA-containing herpes simplex virus. Typically, HSV type II infects the genitalia in an initial primary infection. The virus remains dormant in the dermatomal ganglion cells and periodically presents as recurrent outbreaks of vesicles with viral shedding.

Transmission. Epidemiologic data support the notion that HSV type II is predominantly a sexually transmitted disease. Prepubertal children and celibate adults rarely have antibodies to HSV type II, while antibodies are prevalent among the sexually active adult population (Neinstein et al., 1984).

HSV type II may survive up to 72 hours on dry gauze and for 2 to 4 hours on such fomites as gloves, specula, and toilet seats. No documented infection has been reported from contact with inanimate objects. The predominant mode of spread of HSV type II is by close physical contact, usually sexual in nature (Neinstein et al., 1984).

HSV type I may be found in the genital area as well, although not commonly. This type of HSV infection occurs frequently in nonsexual contact and may find its way to the genital area by autoinoculation.

Clearly, any child who presents with a herpetic infection in the genital area needs to be evaluated for the possibility of sexual abuse (Finkel, 1988a).

Identification. The Tzank prep is quite helpful in identifying HSV and is readily available. The vesicles should be unroofed and a sample of tissue taken by swab at the edge of the vesicles, smeared on a glass slide, and allowed to air dry. Viral culture of the same area is worthwhile and will differentiate between type I and type II. The time from collection to inoculation as well as mode of transport to the lab are important. The infectivity of the specimen for culture will be lost if done later than 4 hours after collection, and sooner if not kept on ice (Murphy, 1983). Some institutions have rapid slides that depend on the skill of the reader and the specimen collector.

Treatment. No medication exists at present that eradicates the virus from the neurons. Symptomatic infections may be treated in adolescents with oral acyclovir. Chronic therapy has been shown to decrease the number of symptomatic days while on suppression therapy. Therapy may decrease the number of recurrences or increase the time between occurrences when off the medication (Straus et al., 1988). Recommendations for children are not available at present.

HIV *Organism.* Caused by the retrovirus known as HIV-1, formerly known as human T-cell lymphotropic virus, type III or HTLV-III, this virus is an RNA-containing virus that contains a reverse transcriptase enzyme that assembles DNA from the genomic RNA (Falloon, Eddy, Weiner, & Pizzo, 1989).

Transmission. Infection with HIV occurs in a number of ways in the pediatric population. The most common means of transmission in children under the age of 13 is vertical transmission from a mother to child through either intrauterine or transplacental means (Falloon et al., 1989). Other forms of transmission commonly seen in adults occur as well, including exposure to contaminated blood or blood products such as coagulation factors, use of needles used by HIV-infected individuals, or sexual contact with HIV-infected people. Clearly, children who experience sexual contact with a perpetrator who is HIV infected are at risk for HIV infection. Credible data are slowly being collected that describe the incidence and risk of HIV infection in children who are sexually abused (Fost, 1990; Gutman et al., 1991; "Suspect HIV Infection," 1988). A recent study of 96 children who tested positive for HIV and who were followed by an acquired immunodeficiency syndrome team revealed that 14 of these children had been sexually abused and in 4 of these children sexual abuse was the source of infection. In an additional 6 cases, sexual abuse was believed to be a probable source. No clear guidelines exist for the testing of sexually abused children for HIV infection (Burgess, Jacobsen, Thompson, Baker, & Grant, 1990; Gellert, Durfee, & Berkowitz, 1990). The clinical situation and HIV status of the perpetrator should weigh in the decision to pursue testing of the child.

Identification. Specific criteria that depend on clinical and laboratory findings are established for the identification of HIV infection in children ("Human Immunodeficiency," 1987). The most frequent laboratory test used to assist in the diagnosis is the relatively sensitive and specific screening ELISA. If warranted, a confirmatory test such as the specific Western blot may be indicated owing to the possibility of false positives and rare false negatives. Recently, antigen-based tests such as polymerase chain reaction (PCR) have been introduced, but these require further standardization (Falloon et al., 1989). The PCR offers the advantage of testing directly for the virus rather than for the antibody to the virus. The antibody test depends on the manufacturing of the protein by the host.

Treatment. The mainstay of management of HIV is early detection and treatment of infections, along with supportive care ("Classification System," 1987). Zidovudine (AZT) as well as other antiviral agents are in various stages of development and trial. AZT shows considerable promise as an inhibitor of viral replication. Its major drawback is dose-dependent hematologic side effects such as macrocytosis, anemia, and neutropenia. Once the child is symptomatic, the length of survival varies from months to years (Falloon et al., 1989).

Pediculosis Pubis

Organism. This condition is caused by the organism *Phthirius pubis*, or "crabs," a relative of the common head lice. The organism has a propensity for warm, moist, hairy areas, such as the groin (Emans & Goldstein, 1982).

Transmission. The organism is transmitted through close physical contact as well as through contact with infested blankets and clothing.

Identification. Pediculosis pubis may be identified through visual inspection of the pubic hair, looking for motile organisms or the eggs, "nits," attached to the hair shaft. Low-power microscopic examination of the hair shaft may be helpful.

Treatment. The mainstay of therapy is a cidal shampoo or lotion such as lindane 1% (Kwell). Shampoo should be lathered into the pubic hair, making sure not to instill shampoo into the urethral meatus. It should be left on for five minutes. After rinsing, the remaining nits should be combed out with a fine-toothed comb. Shaving the pubic area is generally not necessary. The shampoo regimen may be repeated in 7 to 10 days if all nits are not combed out. Infested blankets and clothing should be laundered before being used again.

Gardnerella Vaginalis

Organism. Gardnerella vaginalis, formerly *Haemophilus vaginalis*, can cause a nonspecific vaginitis. It is commonly found in sexually active male and female adolescents. Its presence is more common in sexually abused children than in non-sexually abused controls. *Gardnerella vaginalis* is reported in non-sexually abused children as well as non-sexually active adolescents. It is not pathognomonic of abuse, but its presence in the prepubertal child should arouse suspicion (Jenny, 1990). Bacterial vaginosis, a mixed infection of various microorganisms, including *Gardnerella*, sometimes called nonspecific vaginitis, is described in sexually abused children as well (Centers for Disease Control, 1989).

Transmission. Although *Gardnerella vaginalis* has been reported in nonsexually active children and teens, it is generally considered a sexually transmitted disease, especially in the adult population. Research is necessary to determine its exact mode of transmission in non-sexually abused children. There may be an increase in absolute number that demarcates an infection or an increase in anaerobic bacteria in the vaginal flora (Centers for Disease Control, 1989).

Identification. Presence of *Gardnerella vaginalis* may be suspected by a malodorous, yellow, or white discharge adherent to the vaginal wall. A drop of this discharge suspended in saline on a microscope slide, wet prep, reveals epithelial cells covered with small refractile bacteria, the so-called clue cells. If several drops of 10% potassium hydroxide (KOH) solution are added to the slide, amines may be liberated that will give off a characteristic odor, a positive "whiff test" (Jenny, 1990).

Treatment. The standard treatment for *Gardnerella vaginalis* is with metronidazole:

1. For children less than 45 kilograms:
   metronidazole 5 mg/kilo po TID × 7 days
2. For children 45 kilos or greater and/or in adolescence:
   metronidazole 250 mg po TID × 7 days, or 500 mg po BID × 7 days

Single-dose therapy is not recommended with this infection, secondary to a 40%-60% failure rate.

If metronidazole is contraindicated, clindamycin is a suitable alternative: clindamycin 15 to 25 mg/kilo/24 hr divided in three or four doses for 7 days. In adolescent patients, > 300 mg two times per day for 7 days.

Chancroid and Granuloma Inguinale

These STDs have not been reported in children in the United States (Bell, 1983).

Candida   This is not considered an STD in children or adults, because it is a normal resident in genital and perianal areas (Altchek, 1985).

In Brief
- Any child who presents with an STD needs evaluation for sexual abuse.
- Children with gonorrhea or syphilis outside of the neonatal period have acquired it sexually.
- Children who are sexually abused are at risk for a variety of sexually transmitted diseases.
- Guidelines for the treatment of STDs are available in the American Academy of Pediatrics's *Red Book* or in the Centers for Disease Control's *Morbidity and Mortality Weekly Report* supplements. These sources should be consulted when necessary.
- Identification of the presence of organisms that produce STDs usually requires specific culturing techniques; for example, GC requires chocolate and Thayer-Martin agar as well as a high CO_2 environment; in addition, cotton and cold plates pose a risk to the organism.

7 Mental Health Evaluation

Julie Lippmann
Esther Deblinger

The disclosure of possible child sexual abuse inevitably creates a crisis in the family, a period of some disorganization, and disequilibrium. While this is an unwelcome development for the family, it is useful for health professionals to view such a period as one of great potential for constructive change. Primary care providers, by definition, are on the front lines of service delivery. They may be the first professionals to suspect and officially act upon allegations of child sexual abuse, and therefore may find themselves unwittingly in the midst of such a crisis. In such an uncomfortable position, the natural first impulse is to "triage" the family, as quickly as possible, out to a mental health person to "fix" the situation. In fact, crisis intervention theory recognizes that mental health intervention may be particularly valuable and powerful during a crisis period. Thus the sooner after disclosure the psychologist, psychiatrist, or social worker becomes involved in evaluating the family, the more receptive the family members are likely to be. However, there are certain important steps that the primary care provider can take in making such a referral that can facilitate and ease the process for the family and provide needed information to the mental health evaluator as well.

Referrals　　In making the necessary referrals for a mental health evaluation, the health care professional should explain to the family the reasons for the recommendations. Families are often more receptive to such clarifications from health practitioners than from official investigative personnel. The health care professional should also be prepared to provide a clear and well-documented report of his or her medical evaluation of the child, including both physical findings and interview material, to those who will investigate and provide mental health evaluation of the case. It is critical that all those receiving these reports understand the limits of medical findings, specifically, that they not misconstrue a lack of physical findings to mean that child sexual abuse did not occur.

Legal statutes require professionals with reason to suspect child abuse to report immediately to the child protection agency, which is mandated to investigate alleged abuse by any individual in a caretaking capacity. Ideally, such investigation should be performed jointly by the child protection authorities and the law enforcement system. In cases of extrafamilial abuse—as by a stranger—the case is handled exclusively by the criminal justice system.

Where disclosure results in separation of family members (e.g., removal of a perpetrator), there may be immediate basic needs for shelter, protection, and other material resources. The Department of Social Services is contacted in such cases in order to begin the implementation of required services to sustain a protective environment for the child.

In addition, it is important that the child victim and family be referred to a qualified mental health practitioner for evaluation of the emotional impact of the alleged abuse and recommendations for treatment. The physician should emphasize to the family that child sexual abuse is a trauma that may often have a significant effect on children's emotional development and behavior both now and in the future, even in those situations where there are no physical sequelae, and even if there is no apparent distress at the time. In many cases, psychological evaluation and treatment are ordered by the mandated investigatory agency. In situations where circumstances are ambiguous and may warrant further clarification before the child protective services become involved, the primary care provider may refer directly for mental health assessment. Thus health care professionals must be familiar with the resources in the community for qualified mental health intervention by trained professionals with specific expertise in evaluation and treatment of child sexual abuse. The components of a comprehensive mental health evaluation are described below.

Purpose of the Mental Health Evaluation

Conducting the mental health evaluation in a case of suspected child abuse is a complicated and multifaceted task, involving several distinct but interrelated components and serving at least two different purposes: (a) to make a forensic evaluation and validate the specific allegations of abuse, and (b) to assess the impact of the abuse on the child's overall emotional functioning and make appropriate recommendations for therapeutic intervention with the child and family. In order to fulfill these two functions, the psychologist must combine the primary role of evaluator and fact finder with a therapeutic focus on the protection and ultimate well-being of the child. He or she must provide a supportive and neutral environment in which the child and parents can feel safe enough to disclose necessary information.

Because cases of child sexual abuse typically involve criminal charges against the offender, and often entail civil litigation, the evaluator must be prepared to render an opinion regarding the validity of the child's allegations, the degree of risk, and the traumatization to the child. In order to obtain the evidentiary information needed for such an assessment, the examiner must be neutral and independent of the various parties involved and extremely careful not to contaminate the data by imposing his or her personal biases.

In performing a forensic evaluation, it is crucial that all parties be informed that a report will be generated and will be available to both the local child protective services agency and the county prosecutor's office. The limits of confidentiality in the doctor-patient relationship in circumstances of alleged child abuse should be clearly shared with all parties, including the alleged offender.

Interviewing the Child

A comprehensive psychological evaluation of the alleged victim of child sexual abuse should include the following: identifying information; history of the allegations; characteristics of the alleged abuse and disclosure; developmental, psychosocial, and academic history; family history; history of other childhood traumas; a description of the child's support resources and coping responses; and an assessment of the child's psychiatric functioning prior to, during, and following the alleged abuse. In order to enhance the comprehensiveness and objectivity of the evaluation, the professional should gather this information using multiple sources and multiple methods. For instance, following are some useful sources of information:

- alleged child victim
- child's siblings
- nonoffending guardian(s)
- alleged perpetrator (when possible)
- child protection worker
- prosecutor's office or police investigator
- physician (primary care, emergency room, forensic)
- nurse (school, nurse practitioner, emergency room)
- child's teacher or guidance counselor
- other caretakers (babysitter, grandparent, and so on)

Methods of assessment that may be used in the mental health evaluation include the following:

- interview and observation
- administration of psychological measures
- review of official reports

Validation interviews with an alleged child abuse victim should be conducted in privacy, with the child alone. It may take some time for the evaluator to build the requisite level of rapport and trust with a child who has felt betrayal and to foster a nonthreatening and facilitating climate in which the topic of abuse can be broached and explored in an open-ended and nonjudgmental manner. The evaluator must be attuned to the chronological, as well as the cognitive and emotional, level of development of the child and use skills appropriate to the child's receptive and expressive abilities.

The main sources of information, in addition to the child patient, are his/her family members, including the alleged offender when possible. If the alleged perpetrator is not available for interview or is discouraged from participating by his or her attorney, the evaluator should clearly document this in the report. Furthermore, the report should describe the circumstances and impact of the alleged offender's unavailability on the evaluation.

It is advisable to document behavioral observations as well as the patient's and family members' verbal responses to interview questions. These firsthand observations of symptoms and reactions may serve as important corroboration of others' reports. It is also critical to record information elicited from nonfamily observers, such as the child's teachers, counselors, previous therapists, and/or other caretakers. Whenever possible, all formal records pertinent to the case—including child protection, law enforcement, medical, school, and therapy records— should be obtained for review, with parental permission.

Aspects of Validation

The examiner generally examines the child's presenting symptomatology as well as the family's dynamics. Attention is paid to the specific indicators of the credibility of the child's statements, his or her affect, and presentation style. Clarity, degree of detail of the sexual activity and surrounding circumstances, and the consistency of the allegations are important considerations. Children often initially disclose reluctantly and minimize many aspects of their abusive experiences to avoid distress and embarrassment. Many initially deny or avoid disclosure, or may recant at some point (Sorenson & Snow, 1991). Where the child has described abuse on several different occasions, there may be some inconsistencies in those accounts, especially regarding frequency and severity of the abusive actions. While discrepancies should be clarified, they should not be cause for doubting the child's credibility. The blending of children's abusive experiences and the developmental limitations of their memories may lead to some inconsistencies in recall, particularly with regard to the peripheral details of the alleged abuse.

The examiner looks for congruence between the child's emotions and behavior during disclosure and compares this with the child's affect when discussing more neutral material. However, it should be noted that some sexually abused children suffering from post-traumatic stress disorder (PTSD) may show blunted affect even when discussing their abuse. This is a result of the avoidance and/or affective numbing associated with the disorder. All of these observations must be viewed in the light of developmental expectations. During the course of the evaluation, the child's verbal expressive ability, level of comprehension, memory capacity, suggestibility, and response bias must all be noted. For legal purposes, it is important to discover *who* did *what* to the child, and, within the constraints of the child's developmental ability, *when*, *where*, and *how* the alleged abusive activity may have taken place. The evaluator's main goals are to obtain uncontaminated information from the child by questioning that is as nonleading as possible and to formulate an opinion regarding the veracity of the allegations in an unbiased, open-minded, and independent manner.

Legal and criminal justice professionals caution interviewers not to use focused questions, not to suggest information that is already known, not to indicate any expectations of certain responses, and not to support children in any way for the responses given. Ideally, the more spontaneously the child discusses his or her abuse, the more reliable it is considered to be. Realistically, however, one could wait forever and not get a completely spontaneous disclosure. Some direct questioning is almost always necessary to focus the child's attention on possible abuse-related issues. Initial questioning should be as open-ended and nondirective as possible to elicit free responses. Where such an approach is nonproductive, gradually more focused questions may be posed. When necessary, the evaluator may inquire in a direct but general way about the names, functions, exposure to, and touching of both neutral and sexual body parts without ever introducing the name of the alleged perpetrator (e.g., Has anyone ever touched your _? Have you ever seen anyone else's _?) (Boat & Everson, 1988). In some instances, the interviewer may need to utilize information obtained from other sources to call the child's attention to the critical events or times when the abuse would have been most likely to occur. Very specific questioning, particularly concerning the alleged perpetrator directly, may be used only under extreme circumstances, when other less directive methods have failed and prior information has raised substantial concern for the child's immediate safety. Responses to such potentially leading questions must be very carefully weighed (American Professional Society on the Abuse of Children, 1990) and are less likely to be admissible in court.

Evaluators must be calm in their reactions to children's revelations of abuse. Exhibiting shock, repugnance, or other upset is likely to shut off any further discussion by the child. Differential interest and attention may be considered to convey the interviewer's expectations or encourage or reinforce particular statements. A simple "uh huh" or "and then what happened?" is best. However, it is important to provide a generally supportive, reassuring atmosphere, particularly for the very young child. Bottoms et al. (1989) have demonstrated that such a positive climate can actually enhance the accuracy of very young children's responses, decreasing their errors of commission.

Anatomically correct drawings and anatomically detailed dolls may be useful adjuncts to the interview process to aid young children in communicating their alleged abusive experiences. Such tools are not psychological tests and are not, in themselves, diagnostic of abuse. They must be used with discretion and with appropriate knowledge and training, preferably within the context of a structured interviewing protocol (e.g., Boat & Everson, 1988; White, Strom, & Santilli, 1987). Anatomical drawings and dolls are helpful in identifying body parts and confirming and/or demonstrating abusive activity that has been previously described.

Assessment of Emotional Impact

Information concerning the child's psychiatric history should be obtained directly from the patient, the patient's primary nonoffending caretaker, and the patient's teacher or day-care worker. Multiple sources provide more complete information, as parents are not always aware of their children's unenunciated disturbed thoughts and fears, and children are less likely than parents to describe their own behaviors as disruptive and/or hyperactive.

Standardized measures may be used as adjuncts to clinical interviews to assess more objectively the patient's psychological functioning in relation to the normative population. These measures may be completed by the child, the child's parents, and other caretakers, such as the child's teacher. However, it is important to recognize that there are no empirical data available that link specific psychological test findings with a "diagnosis" of child sexual abuse.

Both the clinical and empirical literatures describe a wide range of psychiatric symptomatology presented by sexually abused children, including regression, anxiety and depressive symptoms, withdrawal, school problems, and acting-out behaviors. Children may have one or several clinical diagnoses or no apparent psychopathology. Thus a comprehensive diagnostic assessment of all psychiatric diagnoses of childhood should be conducted.

Because sexually abused children may meet diagnostic criteria for several disorders, it is important to assess the full range of psychopathology and document all past and present diagnoses. In addition, the evaluator should attempt to ascertain any changes in psychiatric functioning that may be temporally related to the initiation, duration, or termination of the alleged abuse. Psychiatric diagnostic interviews generally cannot stand alone, but must be supplemented by inquiry regarding the child's social and academic functioning as well as questions focusing on specific abuse-related issues and concerns.

Post-Traumatic Stress Disorder

Recent studies have documented a high rate of post-traumatic stress disorder in sexually abused children as well as in adult survivors of childhood incest (Armsworth, 1984; McLeer, Deblinger, Atkins, Foa, & Ralphe, 1988). The clinician assessing a child with a suspected history of sexual abuse needs to explore the presence or absence of these symptoms. In addition, because this disorder can present with a delayed onset and may be chronic or episodic in its course, it is particularly important to assess both past and present episodes and to identify possible triggers for relapse (e.g., contact with perpetrator, court proceedings).

It should be recognized that a diagnosis of PTSD does not prove that the patient has been sexually abused. In fact, Deblinger, McLeer, Atkins, Ralphe, and Foa (1989) conducted a study in which a significant percentage of sexually abused, physically abused, and nonabused child psychiatric inpatients all appeared to experience PTSD symptoms. Clearly, PTSD can be the consequence of many different childhood traumata. However, a careful examination of the specific qualities of PTSD symptoms exhibited may assist the clinician in identifying the nature of the child's trauma. For example, avoidance, a core feature of PTSD, is characteristically demonstrated by children in response to trauma-related stimuli. Therefore, sexually abused children may be more likely to avoid sexualized material than would children who have not been sexually victimized. Likewise, the reexperiencing phenomena exhibited by children suffering PTSD may reflect the specific characteristics of the particular trauma suffered. Thus sexually abused children may evidence repetitive reenactment of their trauma through sexualized doll play.

Inappropriate Sexual Behaviors

Several recent empirical investigations concur that inappropriate sexual behavior may serve as an important psychosocial marker in differentiating sexual abuse victims from other traumatized children (see, e.g., Deblinger et al., 1989; Kolko, Moser, & Weld, 1988). Numerous other reports have identified certain inappropriate sexual behaviors that are more common among sexually abused children than among nonabused children (Friedrich, Beilke, & Urquiza, 1987; Pomeroy, Behar, & Stewart, 1981).

Distinguishing inappropriate from appropriate sexual behaviors in children is sometimes difficult. Children can be expected to show natural curiosity about their own bodies as well as others' bodies. Looking and touching are natural outgrowths of this curiosity. Experimentation with masturbation may also be viewed as a normal and expectable aspect of sexual development.

It is when children exhibit sexual behaviors such as masturbation compulsively and/or in public that such behaviors become inappropriate and problematic. Specifically, preliminary findings reported by Friedrich, Grambach, Broughton, Kruper, and Beilke (1991) suggest that behaviors such as inserting objects in one's vagina or rectum, inserting one's tongue in the mouths of other people, touching other persons' sexual body parts, and imitating intercourse are very rarely exhibited by children who have not been subjected to sexual abuse. Still, it should be recognized that while the observation of these behaviors in children is cause for serious concern and investigation, the behaviors are not alone definitive evidence of abuse. In fact, a child who has been exposed to adult sexual activity in person or through viewing pornographic material may exhibit these sexualized behaviors as well. Careful investigative interviewing, however, can often help to distinguish a sexually abused child from one who has been passively exposed to sexual activity.

Interviewing Other Family Members

A critical phase in the evaluation process involves the interviewing of other family members. The nonoffending parent or parents or other caretakers are interviewed routinely. Whenever possible, the alleged perpetrator should be seen individually as well, particularly if he or she is part of the immediate family. Siblings should also be interviewed to explore their own possible victimization experiences and to obtain their relevant observations of the abusive episodes in question. It is important to remember that sexual abuse is not validated on the basis of particular psychological profiles of the various family members, but rather by integrating all the information obtained throughout the comprehensive evaluation process. A thorough grounding in knowledge about the family is critical to decisions regarding disposition, possible potential placement, and prognosis for treatment. It is necessary to evaluate the extent of parental understanding and support for the child or, perhaps, attitudes of denial, blame, and rejection that may pressure the child to recant or endanger the child.

A more complete understanding of the family's structure and functioning and past and current social circumstances is gained from the nonoffending parent(s). A developmental history of the child is obtained, with attention paid to long-standing cognitive or emotional difficulties that might make a child vulnerable to abuse, and to the parental attitudes toward this child and any problems he or she may have had in the past. The parents' observations concerning the typical behavior of the child and any recent changes in behavior or emotional state are noted. The clinician explores the history of other types of trauma in the family and how they may have been handled. Parental demographic background and personal history are discussed, especially with regard to prior experiences of child sexual abuse, domestic violence, substance abuse or other problems of impulse control, and mental illness. Assessment is made of the parents' overall functioning, including family and social relationships and educational and occupational history.

Nonoffending parents are questioned about their perceptions of family relationships, and specifically about their views of the allegations of abuse. They are asked if there were opportunities for the abuse to have occurred as described. A main goal of this inquiry is to ascertain how the parents are reacting to the allegations of sexual abuse and how helpful they can be to the child. There is no empirically demonstrated "psychological profile" of a typical nonoffending parent, but it is generally agreed that the degree to which a parent can handle the situation and support his or her child is critical in the ultimate outcome of the case.

Recent research has shown that the majority of nonoffending mothers believe their children's allegations (Deblinger, Hathaway, Lippmann, & Steer, submitted; Pierce & Pierce, 1985; Sirles & Frank, 1989) and that their supportive actions may positively influence their children's adjustment (Adams-Tucker, 1981; Conte & Schuerman, 1987). Understandably, a nonoffending parent in the midst of the initial crisis may well need some time to digest and assimilate the implications of the allegations the child has made, and must be willing to make the necessary adjustments to protect and support the child. Rather than assume the collusiveness or denial of a nonoffending parent who may not immediately report or act upon his or her child's disclosure, one must consider the possible motivations, including shame and guilt, fear of retaliation, and financial consequences. However, a nonoffending parent who continues to maintain a guarded and defensive or frankly disbelieving attitude may place his or her child at risk of revictimization. Thus it is important to assess nonoffending family members' responses to the child's allegations over a period of time.

In circumstances where allegations of sexual abuse occur in the context of divorce and custody battles, the credibility of the child's and the nonoffending parent's statements and the possibility that the child may have been "programmed" are often called into question. Such a context does not preclude the likelihood that the allegations are valid, and most professionals feel that instances of intentional programming are rare. A recent study by Thoennes and Tjaden (1990) found that less than 2% of the contested custody/visitation cases they surveyed involved accusations of child sexual abuse—just over half of those allegations against a parent. Approximately half of the allegations were considered by the custody evaluators and/or child protective services to be "substantiated," at a rate consistent with overall substantiation rates not involving custody issues. There is no empirically validated profile of a "programming parent," but in situations where the child's allegations are stated in a rote and seemingly rehearsed fashion, without expectable affect, the examiner should pay attention to certain dynamics on the part of the nonoffending parent. Examples include an absence of emotional distress at the revelation of the abuse and lack of appropriate concern for the child's welfare.

Although there is no complete clinical or psychological testing profile of a sex offender or abusing parent, certain qualities and typologies have been described in the literature. It is helpful to obtain, via clinical interview and/or psychological testing, some sense of the possible perpetrator's own personal history of abuse and victimization; prior criminal, mental health, and substance abuse history; indication of sexual adjustment or dysfunction; and degree of impulse control, narcissism, and sociopathy. The alleged offender's level of social isolation, overall personal and occupational functioning, and coping abilities, as well as recent advent of any potential stressors, should be explored.

It is important to discuss the alleged offender's perception of the nature of family relationships, and specifically the relationship to the child in question. He or she is offered the opportunity to discuss reactions to and alternate explanations for the allegations. For example, a father may play an active role in physical caretaking of a young child, which may account for certain of the child's statements. The clinician should listen for attempts to discredit the child, and for the reasons the alleged offender feels the child would lie. Often, offenders deny the abuse, attempting to protect themselves from losing their jobs and their status in the community and from criminal prosecution and possible imprisonment. They may hope to salvage their families. If abuse is acknowledged, an offender may decline responsibility or rationalize the abuse. Sometimes, for instance, an abuser may attribute sexual activity to the seductiveness of a teenager or the lack of sexual responsiveness of his wife. He may claim he has the right to do what he wants with his child or rationalize the abuse as "sex education." Of course, these common cognitive distortions are never valid excuses for the abuse of a child, but they should be identified as important targets for treatment in the evaluation report.

When an offender has confessed or acknowledged the abuse, either prior to or during the evaluation, the examiner should explore the range of sexual activities in which he or she engaged the child, and his or her methods of engaging and maintaining access to the child. History of abuse of other children and of physical violence toward adults or children should be elicited. The degree to which the offender is willing to accept responsibility and feels remorse and willingness to help the victim is important to the evaluation, as is his or her own motivation to change.

In integrating information from individual sessions with the child, offender, and nonoffending parent(s), it is often helpful to view the family system as a whole and to identify both the strengths and the particular dysfunctional patterns that may have served as homeostatic mechanisms in the family. This is most important in instances of intrafamilial abuse, particularly where the incestuous relationships have been long-standing and ingrained. For example, the instrumental role of an intrafamilial sex offender, perhaps as primary breadwinner, needs to be considered in any adequate assessment of the realistic impact on family functioning of that person's removal and/or incarceration. Blended families appear to be particularly vulnerable to sexual abuse. Finkelhor (1980) found the rate of abuse to be five times as high in these families. Moreover, in Russell's (1986) retrospective study, 17% of women raised with stepfathers reported having been molested by them.

Alliances, boundaries, and power structure within the family warrant consideration. Likewise, the degree of support of extended family and close friends, compared with extreme familial isolation, is an important potential resource. The ability of family members to handle stress and their problematic communication patterns (secretiveness) may be relevant as well.

It is critical to remember that the sexual abuse of children can occur within the context of any family. It is dangerous and unproductive to superimpose stereotypical assumptions about family functioning on the families with which we work. One "classic" pattern that has been discussed frequently in the literature is one in which the mother is in some way absent from the family— whether physically away, working long hours, sick, or debilitated, either physically or emotionally—and unavailable. A particular child, usually a daughter, is recruited as her substitute in household and child-care duties and perhaps in a sexual role with the father as well. There are other such "typical" family structures that have become more or less accepted as descriptive, or even pathognomonic, of "incestuous families." But there are no empirical data to support the universality of these described patterns, and research has demonstrated that such dynamics are, in fact, rare (Deblinger et al., submitted; Salt, Myer, Coleman, & Sauzier, 1990). Moreover, these stereotypes imply an inherent blaming attitude, accusing the nonoffending parent of covert or overt participation in maintaining the incestuous behavior. If the support of the nonoffending parent is most essential in determining the prognosis of the sexually abused child, then an approach that is so condemning of that parent is likely to be counterproductive. Obviously, one must assess each individual case carefully and open-mindedly to determine what is really taking place in that family, and make recommendations for intervention and treatment accordingly.

Feedback and Recommendations for Treatment

After participating in a comprehensive evaluation process, the family deserves some face-to-face feedback and interpretation of the results of the assessment. In validated cases, a clear message of the believability and support of the allegations is crucial for the child, who needs to hear that help is available to him or her and the whole family. The family's reactions to the conclusions and recommendations of the evaluator may be a good predictor of the family's responsiveness to treatment and prognosis. Families' responses may range from acceptance and support of the reality of the abuse, without blaming the child, and acceptance of the responsibility for necessary protection and change, to the opposite extreme of blanket denial of the allegations with resistance and hostility toward an intervention by the system. The latter cases often necessitate removal of the child and placement for protection.

Prognosis

In considering prognosis, it is crucial to recognize that the emotional impact of child sexual abuse varies widely, from apparently negligible or neutral effects to very severe and debilitating ones. Diagnoses extend along a continuum, from no evident symptomatology in approximately 21% of cases (Conte & Schuerman, 1987) to a small but significant minority of cases with resulting multiple personality disorder. Most cases fall somewhere in between, with comprehensive reviews of the literature finding between 46% and 66% of sexually abused children demonstrating significant symptomatology of both internalizing and externalizing nature (Browne & Finkelhor, 1986). The numerous and varied symptoms presented by sexually abused children include sexualized behaviors, fearfulness, avoidance, regression, sleep disturbances, anger, low self-esteem, and depression. With the exception of age-inappropriate sexualized behaviors, these symptoms are not related specifically to sexual abuse but are general indicators of psychological stress. Although there are many exceptions, it is generally felt that children whose abuse has been long-standing, very severe, and perpetrated by a close relative, especially a father, may be more vulnerable to greater psychological problems. Supportive relationships, especially with a nonoffending parent, and generally healthier families are factors that tend to mitigate against severe effects and are predictive of a more positive prognosis (Conte & Schuerman, 1987).

The effects of child sexual abuse are not only problematic in childhood, but appear to be potentially enduring. Adult survivors of child sexual abuse continue to demonstrate significant psychosocial impairment, compared with nonvictimized individuals (Briere & Runtz, 1988). Impairment includes chronic and/or delayed posttraumatic stress symptoms, anxiety and depression, substance abuse, and sexual problems. The research on adult survivors generally focuses on adults who were not treated for their abuse-related difficulties as children, as such treatment was not generally available in the past. Current psychotherapeutic intervention is based largely on the hope that prognosis for individuals treated as children will be better. It is the current generation of child patients who will eventually determine the efficacy of treatment.

Treatment

The variety of differing psychotherapeutic approaches available for treating sexually abused children and their families makes the process of referral confusing at best. The literature includes case studies and clinical anecdotes documenting psychodynamic, insight-oriented, and behavioral methods employed in individual treatment with these children (Becker, Skinner, & Abel, 1982; Van Leevwen, 1988). Group therapy programs, specialized family therapy strategies (Trepper & Barrett, 1989), and comprehensive programs providing multiple treatment modalities offered by multiple therapists (Giarretto, 1982) are also described. However, there have been few attempts to evaluate treatment efficacy empirically using controlled designs and/or standardized outcome measures, and no evidence that clearly supports the efficacy of one of these modalities over the others.

It is not the purpose of this chapter to advocate a particular theoretical orientation or treatment approach. There is growing consensus, however, that, whatever the modality, treatment for child sexual abuse needs to address the issues of abuse directly and thus to encourage the child's uncovering and processing of the events and his or her feelings about them within a safe and supportive therapeutic setting (Friedrich, 1990). In order to assist their children in recovering, nonoffending parents should be involved, at some level, in the treatment process. The therapist should be clear and goal oriented and should have considerable experience and training in child sexual abuse as well as in general child psychology. Specific credentials are generally not as important as experience for performing excellent clinical work. There is currently no official credential for expertise in this field. However, in those cases in which a great deal of legal maneuvering and court testimony are anticipated, it may be wise to select a therapist with a doctorate, licensure, and eligibility to serve as an expert witness.

There is controversy among professionals involved in evaluation and treatment of child sexual abuse about the relative benefits and drawbacks of the same professional performing both evaluation and treatment of a case. On the one hand, some professionals feel that the necessity for objectivity in a forensic, investigatory capacity is inconsistent with the more supportive and therapeutic stance warranted for ongoing treatment. Other complicating factors are the necessity for availability for court testimony and the general limitations of confidentiality, which certainly may affect the ongoing therapeutic relationship. On the other hand, there is much to be said for continuity of care in these delicate cases. Children and their families are necessarily subject to intrusive intervention by a whole variety of parties; they are asked to talk to many strangers about very personal and embarrassing issues. The aim is to minimize the number of such people whom the child and families are asked to trust. Once children have confided the details of their disclosures, they are very sensitive to the reactions of their confidantes. If evaluators then send them off to talk to yet another "helper," the children may feel rejected or be unlikely to continue to talk about these issues. Likewise, families in crisis are particularly open and responsive to those who first reach out to them in a helping way during the crisis period. An attachment is made that can be a powerful therapeutic tool if continuity of care is available. Individual therapists and agencies must weigh the pros and cons in developing their policies and procedures for conducting mental health evaluations in cases of child sexual abuse. Most importantly, however, is the assurance that mental health follow-up be routinely made available to these children and their families.

8 Documentation and Conclusions

Detail of the Medical Record

Meticulous care on the part of the health care professional to make the medical record as detailed and as accurate as possible is imperative to ensure that the best interests of the child are served. The medical record serves as the basis for future discussion of the case. The health care professional should never rely on memory to reconstruct what occurred.

Recording the History

The health care professional performs a vital role in the accurate recording of relevant history and the preservation of evidence in cases of suspected sexual abuse. Because many children do not have physical findings present that are definitive for sexual abuse, substantiation from a legal perspective can be difficult when verbal evidence alone is utilized to meet standards of proof that vary depending upon whether civil or criminal prosecution occurs. The child, by virtue of age, may be unable to testify, or may be so overwhelmed by the process that he or she is intimidated into silence or recantation. Children often have difficulty testifying in a court of law. The statements made to the health care professional by the child can be utilized in court if they are obtained in such a way that they meet the legal hearsay standards. Admissibility of the statements a child makes to a health care professional concerning his or her abuse vary from state to state. Statements made by the child to the health care professional are considered hearsay. Specific legal criteria exist that are applied to decide if the child's statements are in fact admissible evidence in court. In any given case, the judge decides if the manner in which the statements were obtained meet the hearsay rules. All interviews conducted must be done so in a manner that affords the greatest opportunity to enable the statements provided to be admissible evidence.

The judge relies heavily on the health care professional's documentation in the medical record of exactly what questions were asked and the child's verbatim responses. J. E. B. Myers, J.D. (1986), recommends that the examining health care professional be cognizant of the criteria that enable facts to be admissible in court. Myers (1986) encourages the examining health professional to document specific findings in the medical record. The following are criteria that the health care professional should consider during the interview and examination. The health care professional should then document the appropriate findings (Myers, 1986):

1. Document the child's age at the time of the statement.
2. Note the duration of elapsed time between the suspected abuse and the child's statements.
3. Specify who was present when the child made the statement, where the statement was made, and to whom it was made.
4. Document whether specific statements are made in response to questions or are spontaneous.
5. Note whether the child's responses are made to leading or non-leading questions.
6. Note if the child's statement was made at the first opportunity that the child felt safe to talk.
7. Document the emotional state of the child. Note if the child was excited or distressed at the time of the statement and, if so, what signs or symptoms of excitement or distress were observed.
8. Document whether the child was calm, placid, or sleeping prior to making the statement, or soon thereafter.
9. Use the exact words that the child used to describe the characteristics of the event.
10. Document the child's physical condition at the time of the statement.
11. Note any suspected incentives for the child to fabricate or distort the truth.

Recording the Physical Examination

Because the medical record generated from the full evaluation for suspected sexual abuse is open for legal scrutiny, it is imperative to document findings in a manner that will sustain legal scrutiny. Realizing that discrepancies between the physical findings and history of the alleged abuse exist, the health care professional should document findings in a way that leaves open the opportunity to explain any discrepancies. For example, recording the findings of the genital examination simply as "normal" is inappropriate and provides no useful information. Such statements should not appear on the medical record. Rather, a clear description of what was found at the time of the examination should be written in the medical chart. The health care professional should be objective and cognizant of the limitations of the conclusions that can be drawn from the history obtained and examination findings observed. For example, when no acute or chronic signs of trauma are noted on examination, it is inappropriate to state "no evidence of sexual abuse." *Evidence* is a legal term, not a medical term, and should not appear in the medical record. Instead, the health care professional might describe the genital and anal examination in the following manner:

> The child was examined in both the supine frog-leg and knee-chest position. The child is Tanner Stage 1 for both breast and pubic hair and Huffman Stage 1 for estrogenization of external genitalia; the labia minora and majora are well formed and without acute or chronic signs of trauma; hymenal membrane has a crescentic-shaped orifice, with a thin velamentous border and a transverse diameter measuring 3-5 mm with labial separation and traction; the external surface of the hymenal membrane, fossa navicularis, and posterior fourchette do not demonstrate any acute or chronic signs of injury; there is no abnormal degree of redness, vaginal discharge, odor, or stigmata of sexually transmitted disease.
>
> The external anal verge tissues were examined in the knee-chest position. There was a symmetric rugal pattern, normal sphincter tone, normal response to traction, no postinflammatory pigmentary changes, no unusual venous pattern, and no signs of acute or chronic signs of injury noted.

When neither acute nor chronic findings of trauma are present, the medical record establishes baseline documentation of the child's anogenital anatomy. This detailed documentation of the child's anogenital anatomy, by written description, hand drawing, or photograph, will allow comparison and possible observation of changes if new allegations arise at a later date.

It is important to remember that no residual findings are anticipated when a child has been fondled in an atraumatic manner or is evaluated weeks after the last inappropriate contact, even if a history suggestive of superficial injuries has been provided. Therefore, it is best for the health care professional to describe what is found and draw conclusions that place all findings in the proper context. Examples include the following:

1. Delineation of specific alleged acts with specific physical findings with either acute or chronic residual might be stated as follows: The physical findings of . . . are residual to the alleged events as reflected by the history provided by the child.
2. Description of an examination that demonstrates no acute or chronic residual when a history of fondling and oral-genital activities has been provided might be as follows: The physical examination does not demonstrate residual to the alleged events, nor would it be anticipated to, based on the history of the inappropriate contact provided by the child.
3. Description of physical findings that are discrepant with the history provided (e.g., the findings of a straddle injury are different from those expected from a penetration injury) might be as follows: The physical examination findings do not reflect a pattern of injury anticipated by the history provided by the child.

With these examples as a guide, the examining health care professional should have enough options available to describe the examination findings accurately and draw a conclusion without confusing the situation. A medical record that is accurate and detailed will serve both the examiner and the child when the examiner is asked to recount the details of the interview or physical examination.

Table 8.1, which is adapted from the AAP Committee on Child Abuse and Neglect's "Guidelines for the Evaluation of Sexual Abuse of Children" (1991), offers advice prepared by the committee with regard to the health care professional's making a decision to report a case in which sexual abuse is suspected.

Court Testimony   The health care professional involved in a sexual abuse evaluation may be asked to appear in the courtroom in either of two capacities (Torrey & Ludwig, 1987). First, the health care professional may be asked to establish an official record of the diagnosis, treatment, and implication of an injury. In this instance, the health care professional serves as a "fact" witness. Second, the health care professional may be asked to testify in an expert capacity. As such, he or she may be asked to render an opinion

TABLE 8.1 Guidelines for Making the Decision to Report Sexual Abuse of Children

| | Data Available | | | Response | |
	Physical	Laboratory	Level of Concern About Sexual Abuse	Action
History				
None	Normal examination	None	None	None
Behavioral changes	Normal examination	None	Low (worry)	± Report[a]; follow closely (possible mental health referral)
None	Nonspecific findings	None	Low (worry)	± Report[a]; follow closely
Nonspecific history by child or history by parent only	Nonspecific findings	None	Possible (suspect)	± Report[a]; follow closely
None	Specific findings	None	Probable	Report
Clear statement	Normal examination	None	Probable	Report
Clear statement	Specific findings	None	Probable	Report
None	Normal examination, nonspecific or specific findings	Positive culture for gonorrhea; positive serologic test for syphilis; presence of semen, sperm, acid phosphatase	Definite	Report
Behavioral changes	Nonspecific changes	Other sexually transmitted diseases	Probable	Report

SOURCE: AAP Committee on Child Abuse and Neglect (1991, p. 257). Reproduced by permission of *Pediatrics*, Vol. 87, p. 254. Copyright 1991.
a. A report may or may not be indicated. The decision to report should be based on discussion with local or regional experts and/or child protective services agencies.

concerning the likely cause of various findings and may be asked to interpret technical material for the court. In this situation, the health care professional serves as an "expert" witness.

Typically, the health care professional involved with a sexual abuse case will be serving in the role of a fact witness. Prior to the court appearance, the health care professional should determine how the medical testimony will be used in the case through discussions with the attorneys involved. The professional should review the record for the case. Some familiarity with the case is helpful, however, the testimony does not have to be rendered from memory; on the witness stand, the health care professional may refer to the record when necessary.

Attorneys from both prosecution and defense will have the opportunity to question the witness. During direct examination, the prosecuting attorney will present the information relevant to the case and call upon the health care professional to confirm certain facts and draw conclusions. Absolute answers are rarely required, and the health care professional should never conclude that only one particular explanation is possible. However, he or she may state the most likely cause for a given finding.

During cross-examination, the defense attorney may challenge the statements made by the prosecution and the health care professional. This may be an anxiety-provoking experience. If the witness is asked a question that he or she feels unable to answer, the witness should state so. If a question is asked in a yes/no format and the health care professional feels that it cannot be answered with that kind of response, he or she should state this and turn to the judge, providing certain qualifications while answering. If a question is so complex that it is unclear, the health care professional should ask for a restatement of the question. At times, the attorney may paraphrase statements made by the health care professional, who should then correct any misstatements.

Figure 8.1 depicts the legal and social services approach to a sexual abuse complaint once a report is made (Miller, 1987). It serves as a reference for how an abuse case travels through the judicial and social service systems.

Conclusion

Sexual abuse of children is a complex form of victimization that requires a multidisciplinary approach during initial evaluation and treatment. The goal of any intervention is to protect the child and, if possible, correct the environment that allowed the abuse to occur or continue. The health care professional is called upon to identify suspected cases, to interview the patient,

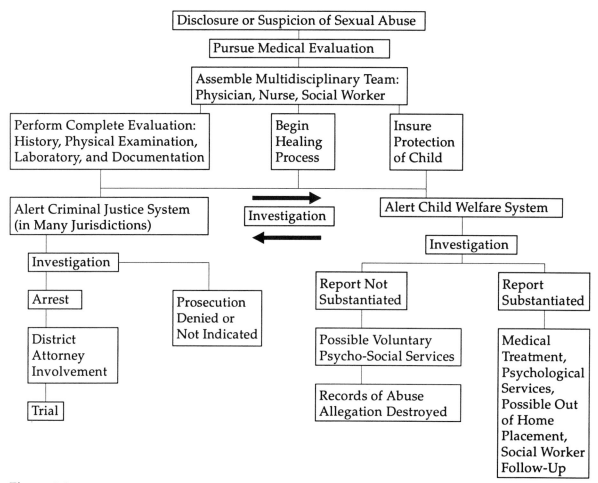

Figure 8.1
Entrance of a Case Into the Child Welfare or Legal System
Adapted from Miller (1987). Used by permission of the author.

and to examine the patient for any signs of abuse. In addition, the health care professional is expected to function as an objective advocate for the child and to work toward a therapeutic resolution. Health care professionals need to avail themselves of relevant information on patterns of victimization, medical and mental health residual to victimization, and therapeutic approaches to meet both short- and long-term needs of the child and family. Health care professionals should actively participate with the multidisciplinary teams in their communities.

We anticipate that health care professionals, after reading this manual, will be more comfortable with the evaluation of children suspected of being sexually abused. The health care professional should come to realize the importance of the history, the relative lack of physical findings, and the importance of clearly written and documented medical records from the standpoint of serving these children's best interests. The forensic medical evaluation of the sexually abused child is a relatively new and rapidly maturing field. The health care professional must keep up to date with the evolving literature as new insights into the needs of victimized children are reported.

In Brief

Do's
- Describe findings simply and clearly.
- Be aware of the child's developmental status.
- Define the child's language and use a common vocabulary.
- Use exact words in the documentation.
- Use nonleading questions during the interview.
- Record questions asked of the child and the specific answers given.
- Use diagrams or photographs to supplement the written documentation.

Don'ts
- Don't use leading questions if at all possible.
- Don't rely on memory; rather, compile a well-documented chart that can be consulted later for details.
- Don't use the terms *virginal* or *intact* hymen.
- Don't say "no evidence for abuse" in the documentation.
- Don't draw absolute conclusions.

References

Adams, J. A., & Horton, M. (1989). Clinical experiences: Is it sexual abuse? *Clinical Pediatrics, 28,* 146-148.

Adams-Tucker, C. (1981). A socioclinical overview of 28 sex-abused children. *Child Abuse & Neglect, 5,* 361-376.

Alexander, R. C. (1990). Education of the physician in child abuse. *Pediatric Clinics of North America, 37,* 971-988.

Altchek, A. (1972). Pediatric vulvovaginitis. *Pediatric Clinics of North America, 19,* 559-580.

Altchek, A. (1985). Recognizing and controlling vulvovaginitis in children. *Contemporary Pediatrics, 2,* 59-70.

American Academy of Pediatrics (AAP), Committee on Child Abuse and Neglect. (1991). Guidelines for the evaluation of sexual abuse of children. *Pediatrics, 87,* 254-260.

American Academy of Pediatrics (AAP), Committee on Early Childhood, Adoption, and Dependent Care. (1983). Gonorrhea in pre-pubertal children. *Pediatrics, 71,* 553.

American Professional Society on the Abuse of Children. (1990). *Guidelines for psychosocial evaluation of suspected sexual abuse in young children.* Chicago: Author.

Armsworth, M. (1984). Post-traumatic stress response in women who experienced incest as children or adolescents. *Dissertation Abstracts International, 46*(5B), 1674.

Bachmann, G. A., Moeller, T. P., & Benett, J. (1988). Childhood sexual abuse and the consequences in adult women. *Obstetrics and Gynecology, 71,* 631-642.

Baker R. (1986). Seat belt injury masquerading as sexual abuse. *Pediatrics, 77,* 435.

Barton, D. J., Sloan, G. M., Nichter, L. S., & Reinisch, J. F. (1988). Hair-thread tourniquet syndrome. *Pediatrics, 82,* 925-928.

Bays, J., & Jenny, C. (1990). Genital and anal conditions confused with child sexual abuse trauma. *American Journal of Diseases of Children, 144,* 1319-1322.

Becker, J., Skinner, H., & Abel, G. (1982). Treatment of a four year old child victim of incest. *American Journal of Family Therapy, 10,* 41-46.

Behrman, R. E., & Kliegman, R. M. (1983). The fetus and the neonatal infant: Physical examination of the newborn infant. In R. E. Behrman & V. C. Vaughan (Eds.), *Nelson textbook of pediatrics* (12th ed., pp. 322-416). Philadelphia: W. B. Saunders.

Bell, T. A. (1983). Major sexually transmitted diseases in children and adolescents. *Pediatric Infectious Disease, 2,* 153-161.

Berkowitz, C. D., Elvik, S. L., & Logan, M. K. (1987a). Labial fusion in prepubescent girls: A marker for sexual abuse? *American Journal of Obstetrics and Gynecology, 156,* 16.

Berkowitz, C. D., Elvik, S. L., & Logan, M. K. (1987b). A simulated "acquired" imperforate hymen following the genital trauma of sexual abuse. *Clinical Pediatrics, 26,* 307-309.

Berth-Jones, J., Graham-Brown, R. A. C., & Burns, D. A. (1989). Lichen sclerosus. *Archives of Diseases of Children, 64,* 1204-1206.

Blumberg, M. L. (1978, March). Child sexual abuse: Ultimate in maltreatment syndrome. *New York State Journal of Medicine,* pp. 612-616.

Boat, B. W., & Everson, M. D. (1988). Interviewing young children with anatomical dolls. *Child Welfare, 67,* 337-352.

Bottoms, B. L., Goodman, G. S., Rudy, L., Port, L., England, P., Aman, C., & Wilson, M. E. (1989, August). *Children's testimony for a stressful event: Improving children's reports.* Paper presented at the 97th Annual Meeting of the American Psychological Association, New Orleans.

Branch, G., & Paxton, R. (1965). A study of gonococcal infections among infants and children. *Public Health Reports, 80,* 347-352.

Breen, J. L., & Maxson, W. S. (1977). Ovarian tumors in children and adolescents. *Clinical Obstetrics and Gynecology, 20,* 607-623.

Briere, J., & Runtz, M. (1988). Symptomatology associated with childhood sexual victimization in a nonclinical adult sample. *Child Abuse & Neglect, 12,* 51-59.

Browne, A., & Finkelhor, D. (1986). Impact of child sexual abuse: A review of the research. *Psychological Bulletin, 99,* 66-77.

Burgess, A. W., & Holmstrom, L. L. (1975). Sexual trauma of children and adolescents: Pressure, sex, secrecy. *Nursing Clinics of North America, 10,* 551-563.

Burgess, A. W., Jacobsen, B., Thompson, J. E., Baker, T., & Grant, C. A. (1990). HIV testing of sexual assault populations: Ethical and legal issues. *Journal of Emergency Nursing, 16,* 331-338.

Cantwell, H. B. (1987). Update on vaginal inspection as it relates to child sexual abuse in girls under thirteen. *Child Abuse & Neglect, 11,* 545-546.

Centers for Disease Control (CDC). (1989). Sexually transmitted diseases treatment guidelines. *Morbidity and Mortality Weekly Report, 38*(Suppl. 8), 1-43.

Classification system for human immunodeficiency virus (HIV) infection in children under 13 years of age. (1987, April 24). *Morbidity and Mortality Weekly Report,* p. 36.

Clayden, G. (1987). Anal appearances and child sex abuse. *Lancet, 1,* 620-621.

Coffman, K. B., Boyce, W. T., & Hansen, R. C. (1985). Phytodermatitis simulating child abuse. *American Journal of Diseases of Children, 139,* 229-240.

Conte, J. R., & Schuerman, J. R. (1987). Factors associated with an increased impact of child sexual abuse. *Child Abuse & Neglect, 11,* 201-211.

Dannaker, C. J., Glover, R. A., & Goltz, R. W. (1988). Phytodermatitis: A mystery case report. *Clinical Pediatrics, 27,* 289-290.

Deblinger, E., Hathaway, C. R., Lippmann, J., & Steer, R. (1992). *Psychosocial correlates of symptom distress in nonoffending mothers of suspected victims of sexual abuse.* Manuscript submitted for publication.

Deblinger, E., McLeer, S. V., Atkins, M. S., Ralphe, D., & Foa, E. (1992). Post traumatic stress in sexually abused, physically abused and non-abused children. *Child Abuse & Neglect, 13,* 403-408.

DeFrancis, V. (1969). *Protecting the child victim of sex crime.* Denver, CO: American Humane Association.

De Jong, A. R. (1985). The medical evaluation of sexual abuse in children. *Hospital and Community Psychiatry, 36,* 509-512.

De Jong, A. R. (1988). *Evidence collection and secretion analysis.* Unpublished manuscript, Thomas Jefferson University College of Medicine, Philadelphia.

De Jong, A. R., Hervada, A. R., & Emmett, G. A. (1983). Epidemiologic variations in childhood sexual abuse. *Child Abuse & Neglect, 7,* 155-162.

De Jong, A. R., & Rose, M. (1989). Frequency and significance of physical evidence in legally proven cases of child sexual abuse. *Pediatrics, 84,* 1022-1026.

De Jong, A. R., & Rose, M. (1991). Legal proof of child sexual abuse in the absence of physical evidence. *Pediatrics, 88,* 506-511.

De Jong, A. R., Weiss, J. C., & Brent, R. F. (1982). Condyloma acuminata in children. *American Journal of Diseases of Children, 136,* 704-706.

Dodson, A. I. (1970). *Urological surgery.* St. Louis: C. V. Mosby.

Dubowitz, H. (1988). Child abuse programs and pediatric residency training. *Pediatrics, 82,* 477-480.

Emans, S. J. (1986). Vulvovaginitis in the child and adolescent. *Pediatrics in Review, 8,* 12-19.

Emans, S. J. H., & Goldstein, D. P. (1982). *Pediatric and adolescent gynecology* (2nd ed.). Boston: Little, Brown.

Emans, S. J. H., & Goldstein, D. P. (1990). *Pediatric and adolescent gynecology* (3rd ed). Boston: Little, Brown.

Emans, S. J. H., Woods, E. R., Flagg, N. J., & Freeman, A. (1987). Genital findings in sexually abused, symptomatic and asymptomatic girls. *Pediatrics, 79,* 778-785.

Faller, K. C. (1988). *Child sexual abuse: An interdisciplinary manual for diagnosis, case management, and treatment.* New York: Columbia University Press.

Faller, K. C. (1990a). Types of questions for children alleged to have been sexually abused. *Advisor, 3,* 3-5.

Faller, K. C. (1990b). *Understanding child sexual maltreatment.* Newbury Park, CA: Sage.

Falloon, J., Eddy, J., Weiner, L., & Pizzo, P. A. (1989). Human immunodeficiency virus infection in children. *Journal of Pediatrics, 114,* 1-23.

Feldman, W., Feldman, E., Goodman, J. T., McGrath, J. P., Pless, R. P., Corsini, L., & Bennett, S. (1991). Is childhood sexual abuse really increasing in prevalence? An analysis of the evidence. *Pediatrics, 88,* 29-33.

Fink, C. W. (1983). A perianal rash in Kawasaki disease. *Pediatric Infectious Disease, 2,* 140-141.

Finkel, M. A. (1988a). The medical evaluation of child sexual abuse. In D. H. Schetry & A. H. Green (Eds.), *Child sexual abuse: A handbook for healthcare and legal professionals* (pp. 82-103). New York: Brunner/Mazel.

Finkel, M. A. (1988b). Medical examination in alleged sexual abuse of children. In Governor's Task Force on Child Abuse, *Child abuse: A professional's guide to the identification, reporting, investigation and treatment.* Trenton, NJ: Governor's Task Force on Child Abuse.

Finkel, M. A. (1989). Anogenital trauma in sexually abused children. *Pediatrics, 84,* 317-322.

Finkel, M. A. (1992). *Post-fondling dysuria in sexually abused children.* Manuscript submitted for publication.

Finkelhor, D. (1979). *Sexually victimized children.* New York: Free Press.

Finkelhor, D. (1980). Risk factors in the sexual abuse of children. *Child Abuse & Neglect, 4,* 265-273.

Finkelhor, D. (1984). *Child sexual abuse: New theory and research.* New York: Free Press.

Finkelhor, D., & Associates. (1986). *A sourcebook on child sexual abuse.* Beverly Hills, CA: Sage.

Finkelhor D., & Hotaling, G. T. (1983, July). *Sexual abuse in the National Incidence Study of Child Abuse and Neglect.* Final report for grant 90-CA840/01 from the National Center on Child Abuse and Neglect.

Finkelhor, D., Hotaling, G., Lewis, I. A., & Smith C. (1990). Sexual abuse in a national survey of adult men and women: Prevalence, characteristics, and risk factors. *Child Abuse & Neglect, 14,* 19-28.

Fleisher, G. F., & Ludwig, S. (1988). *Textbook of pediatric emergency medicine* (2nd ed.). Baltimore: Williams & Wilkins.

Fost, N. (1990). Ethical considerations in testing victims of sexual abuse for HIV infection. *Child Abuse & Neglect, 14,* 5-7.

Friedrich, W. N. (1990). *Psychotherapy of sexually abused children and their families.* New York: W. W. Norton.

Friedrich, W. N., Beilke, R. L., & Urquiza, A. J. (1987). Children from sexually abusive families: A behavioral comparison. *Journal of Interpersonal Violence, 2,* 391-402.

Friedrich, W. N., Grambach, A., Broughton, D., Kruper, J., & Beilke, R. L. (1991). Normative sexual behavior in children. *Pediatrics, 88,* 456-464.

Fromuth, M. E. (1983). *The long term psychological impact of childhood sexual abuse.* Unpublished doctoral dissertation, Auburn University.

Gellert, G. A., Durfee, M. J., & Berkowitz, C. D. (1990). Developing guidelines for HIV antibody testing among victims of pediatric sexual abuse. *Child Abuse & Neglect, 14,* 9-17.

Giarretto, H. (1982). A comprehensive child sexual abuse treatment program. *Child Abuse & Neglect, 6,* 263-278.

Gill, F. T. (1989). Caring for abused children in the emergency department. *Holistic Nursing Practice, 4*, 37-43.

Goldberg, C. C., & Yates, A. (1990). The use of anatomically correct dolls in the evaluation of sexually abused children. *American Journal of Diseases of Children, 144*, 1334-1336.

Gordon, I. B. (1983). Pediatric gynecology and adolescent issues: Infections and shin disorders of the genitalia. In R. E. Behrman & V. C. Vaughan (Eds.), *Nelson textbook of pediatrics* (12th ed., pp. 1515-1530). Philadelphia: W. B. Saunders.

Gutman, L. T., St. Claire, K. K., Weedy, C., Herman-Giddens, M. E., Lane, B. A., & Niemeyer, J. G. (1991). Human immunodeficiency virus transmission by child sexual abuse. *American Journal of Diseases of Children, 145*, 137-141.

Heger, A., & Emans, S. J. (1990). Introital diameter as the criterion for sexual abuse. *Pediatrics, 85*, 222-223.

Herman-Giddens, M., & Frothingham, T. E. (1987). Prepubertal female genitalia: Examination for evidence of sexual abuse. *Pediatrics, 80*, 203-208.

Hibbard, R. A., & Zollinger, T. W. (1990). Patterns of child sexual abuse knowledge among professionals. *Child Abuse & Neglect, 14*, 347-355.

Hobbs, C. J., & Wynne, J. M. (1987). Differential diagnosis in child sexual abuse [Letter to the editor]. *Lancet, 1*, 510.

Horowitz, D. A. (1987). Physical examination of sexually abused children and adolescents. *Pediatrics in Review, 9*, 25-29.

Huffman, J. W. (1969). *The gynecology of childhood and adolescence*. Philadelphia: W. B. Saunders.

Human immunodeficiency virus infection. (1987). *Morbidity and Mortality Weekly Report, 36*, 225-236.

Jason, J., Williams, S. L., Burton, A., & Rochat, R. (1982). Epidemiologic differences between sexual and physical child abuse. *Journal of the American Medical Association, 247*, 3344-3348.

Jenny, C. (1990). Child sexual abuse and STD. In K. K. Holmes, P. Mardh, P. F. Sparling, & P. J. Wiesner (Eds.), *Sexually transmitted diseases* (2nd ed., pp. 1109-1112). New York: McGraw-Hill.

Jenny, C., Sutherland, S. E., & Sandahl, B. B. (1986). Developmental approach to preventing the sexual abuse of children. *Pediatrics, 78*, 1034-1038.

Johnson, C. F. (1991). Prolapse of urethra: Confusion of clinical and anatomic traits with sexual abuse. *Pediatrics, 87*, 722-725.

Josephson, G. W. (1979). The male rape victim: Evaluation and treatment. *Journal of American College of Emergency Physicians, 8*, 13-15.

Kempe, C. H. (1978). Sexual abuse, another hidden pediatric problem: The 1977 C. Anderson Aldrich Lecture. *Pediatrics, 62*, 382-389.

Kempe, C. H. (1980). Incest and other forms of sexual abuse. In C. H. Kempe & R. E. Helfer (Eds.), *The battered child* (3rd ed.) pp. 198-214. Chicago: University of Chicago Press.

Kempe, C. H., Silverman, F. N., Steele, B. F., Droegemueller, W., & Silver, H. K. (1962). The battered-child syndrome. *Journal of the American Medical Association, 181*, 17-24.

Kirschner, R. H., & Stein, R. J. (1985). The mistaken diagnosis of child abuse: A form of medical abuse? *American Journal of Diseases of Children, 139*, 873-875.

Klevan, J. L., & De Jong, A. R. (1990). Urinary tract symptoms and urinary tract infection following sexual abuse. *American Journal of Diseases of Children, 144*, 242-244.

Kolko, D. J., Moser, J. T., & Weld, S. R. (1988). Behavioral/emotional indicators of sexual abuse in child psychiatric inpatients: A controlled comparison with physical abuse. *Child Abuse & Neglect, 12*, 529-541.

Krugman, R. D. (1986). Recognition of sexual abuse in children. *Pediatrics in Review, 8*, 25-30.

Ladson, S., Johnson, C. F., & Doty, R. E. (1987). Do physicians recognize sexual abuse? *American Journal of Diseases of Children, 141*, 411-415.

Laymon, C. W., & Freeman, C. (1944). Relationship of balantis xerotica obliterans to lichen sclerosis et atrophicus. *Archives of Dermatology, 49*, 57-59.

Leventhal, J. M., Hamilton, J., Rekedal, S., Tebano-Micci, A., & Eyster, C. (1989). Anatomically correct dolls used in interviews of young children suspected of having been sexually abused. *Pediatrics, 84*, 900-906.

Levin, A. V., & Selbst, S. M. (1988). Vulvar hemangioma simulating child abuse. *Clinical Pediatrics, 27*, 213-215.

Lindberg, F. H., & Distad, L. J. (1985). Post-traumatic stress disorders in women who experienced childhood incest. *Child Abuse & Neglect, 9*, 329-334.

Loening-Baucke, V. (1991). Lichen sclerosis et atrophicus in children. *American Journal of Diseases of Children, 145,* 1058-1061.

Lowe, F. C., Hill, G. S., Jeffs, R. D., & Brendler, C. B. (1986). Urethral prolapse in children: Insights into etiology and management. *Journal of Urology, 135,* 100-103.

Ludwig, S. (1988). Psychosocial emergencies: Child abuse. In G. R. Fleisher & S. Ludwig, *Textbook of pediatric emergency medicine* (2nd ed.) pp. 1127-1163. Baltimore: Williams & Wilkins.

Marshall, W. N., Puls, T., & Davidson, C. (1988). New child abuse spectrum in an era of increased awareness. *American Journal of Diseases of Children, 142,* 664-667.

McCann, J., Pearlman, L. A., Sakheim, D. K., & Abrahamson, D. J. (1988). Assessment and treatment of the adult survivor of childhood sexual abuse within a schema framework. In S. M. Sgroi (Ed.), *Vulnerable populations* (Vol. 1, pp. 77-101). Lexington, MA: Lexington.

McCann, J., Voris, J., & Simon, M. A. (1988). Labial adhesions and posterior fourchette injuries in childhood sexual abuse. *American Journal of Diseases of Children, 142,* 659-663.

McCann, J., Voris, J., Simon, M. A., & Wells, R. (1990). Comparison of genital examination techniques in prepubertal girls. *Pediatrics, 85,* 182-187.

McLeer, S. V., Deblinger, E., Atkins, M., Foa, E., & Ralphe, D. (1988). Post-traumatic stress disorder in sexually abused children: A prospective study. *Journal of the American Academy of Child and Adolescent Psychiatry, 27,* 650-654.

Merz, B. (1988). Medical news and perspectives: DNA probes for papillomavirus strains readied for cervical cancer screening [Letter to the editor]. *Journal of the American Medical Association, 260,* 2777.

Miller, S. K. (1987). *Workbook on child abuse.* Unpublished manuscript, Children's Hospital of Philadelphia.

Ming, J. S. L. (1990). Responsibilities of primary care providers in child sexual abuse. *Nurse Practitioner Forum, 1,* 90-97.

Morrow, G. (1988). Residency training in management of child abuse. *Pediatrics, 82,* 513-514.

Muram, D. (1989). Child sexual abuse: Relationship between sexual acts and genital findings. *Child Abuse & Neglect, 13,* 211-216.

Murphy, M. D. (1983). Office laboratory diagnosis of sexually transmitted diseases. *Pediatric Infectious Disease, 2,* 146-152.

Murphy, T. V., & Nelson, J. D. (1979). Shigella vaginitis: Results of 38 patients and review of the literature. *Pediatrics, 63,* 511-516.

Myers, J. E. B. (1986). Role of physicians in preserving verbal evidence of child abuse. *Journal of Pediatrics, 109,* 409-411.

Neinstein, L. S., Goldenring, J., & Carpenter, S. (1984). Nonsexual transmission of sexually transmitted disease: An infrequent occurrence. *Pediatrics, 74,* 67-76.

Paradise, J. E. (1990). The medical evaluation of the sexually abused child. *Pediatric Clinics of North America, 374,* 839-861.

Paradise, J. E., Campos, J. M., Friedman, H. M., & Frishmuth, G. (1982). Vulvovaginitis in premenstrual girls: Clinical features and diagnostic evaluation. *Pediatrics, 70,* 193-198.

Paradise, J. E., Rostain, A. L., & Nathanson, M. (1988). Substantiation of sexual abuse charges when parents dispute custody or visitation. *Pediatrics, 81,* 835-839.

Paradise, J. E., & Willis, E. D. (1985). Probability of vaginal foreign body in girls with genital complaints. *American Journal of Diseases of Children, 139,* 472.

Peters, S. D., Wyatt, G. E., & Finkelhor, D. (1986). Prevalence. In D. Finkelhor & Associates, *A sourcebook on child sexual abuse* (pp. 15-59). Beverly Hills, CA: Sage.

Pierce, R., & Pierce, L. (1985). The sexually abused child: A comparison of male and female victims. *Child Abuse & Neglect, 9,* 191-199.

Pomeroy, J. C., Behar, D., & Stewart, D. C. (1981). Abnormal sexual behavior in pre-pubescent children. *British Journal of Psychiatry, 138,* 119-125.

Porter, F. S., Blick, L. C., & Sgroi, S. M. (1982). Treatment of the sexually abused child. In S. M. Sgroi (Ed.), *Handbook of clinical intervention in child sexual abuse* (pp. 109-145). Lexington, MA: Lexington.

Press, S., Schachner, L., & Paul, P. (1980). Clitoris tourniquet syndrome. *Pediatrics, 66,* 781.

Reinhart, M. A. (1987). Sexual abuse of battered young children. *Pediatric Emergency Care, 3,* 36-38.

Ricci, L. R. (1991). Photographing the physically abused child: Principles and practice. *American Journal of Diseases of Children, 145,* 275-281.

Rickwood, A. M. K., Hemalatha, V., Batcup, G., & Spitz, L. (1980). Phimosis in boys. *British Journal of Urology, 52,* 147-150.

Rimza, M. E., & Niggemann, E. H. (1982). Medical evaluation of sexually abused children: A review of 311 cases. *Pediatrics, 69,* 8-14.

Russell, D. E. H. (1983). The incidence and prevalence of intrafamilial and extrafamilial sexual abuse of female children. *Child Abuse & Neglect, 7,* 133-146.

Russell, D. E. H. (1986). *The secret trauma: Incest in the lives of girls and women.* New York: Basic Books.

Salt, P., Myer, M., Coleman, L., & Sauzier, M. (1990). The myth of the mother as "accomplice" to the child sexual abuse. In B. Gomes-Schwartz, J. M. Horowitz, & A. P. Cardarelli (Eds.), *Child sexual abuse: The initial effects.* Newbury Park, CA: Sage.

Saywitz, K. J. (1990). Developmental considerations for forensic interviewing. *The Interviewer, 3*(2), 2, 5, 15.

Schoon, D. L. (1988). Practical pediatrics: Reader's view on masturbation [Letter to the editor]. *Pediatric News, 22,* 41.

Seidel, J. S., Elvik, S. L., Berkowitz, C. D., & Day, C. (1986). Presentation and evaluation of sexual misuse in the emergency department. *Pediatric Emergency Care, 2,* 157-164.

Seidl, T. (1987, June). Constructively assessing child sexual abuse. In A. E. Mauro & L. M. Mauro (Eds.), *Critical issues in responding to child abuse in the 1980's.* Philadelphia: Temple University, Center for Social Policy and Community Development.

Seidl, T. (1992). Special interviewing techniques. In S. Ludwig & A. E. Kornberg (Eds.), *Child abuse: A medical reference* (2nd ed., pp. 279-293). New York: Churchill Livingstone.

Seidl, T., & Paradise, J. E. (1984). Child sexual abuse: Effective case management by a multidisciplinary team. *Resident and Staff Physician, 30,* 48-51.

Sgroi, S. M. (1975). Sexual molestation of children: The last frontier in child abuse. *Children Today, 4,* 18-21, 44.

Sgroi, S. M. (Ed.). (1982). *Handbook of clinical intervention in child sexual abuse.* Lexington, MA: Lexington.

Sgroi, S. M., Blick, L. C., & Porter, F. S. (1982). A conceptual framework for child sexual abuse. In S. M. Sgroi (Ed.), *Handbook of clinical intervention in child sexual abuse* (pp. 9-37). Lexington, MA: Lexington.

Sgroi, S. M., & Bunk, B. S. (1988). A clinical approach to adult survivors of child sexual abuse. In S. M. Sgroi (Ed.), *Vulnerable populations* (Vol. 1, pp. 137-186). Lexington, MA: Lexington.

Shore, W., & Winkelstein, J. (1971). Non-venereal transmission of gonococcal infections to children. *Journal of Pediatrics, 79,* 661-663.

Singh, B., Kim, H., & Wax, S. H. (1978). Strangulation of glans penis by hair. *Urology, 11,* 170-173.

Sirles, E., & Frank, P. (1989). Factors influencing mothers' reactions to intrafamilial sexual abuse. *Child Abuse & Neglect, 13,* 131-139.

Sorenson, T., & Snow, B. (1991). How children tell: The process of disclosure in child sexual abuse. *Child Welfare, 70,* 3-15.

Spear, R. M., Rothbaum, R. J., Keating, J. P., Blaufuss, M. C., & Rosenblum, J. L. (1985). Perianal streptococcal cellulitis. *Journal of Pediatrics, 107,* 557-559.

Straus, S. E., Croen, K. D., Sawyer, M. E., Freifeld, A. G., Felser, J. M., Dale, J. K., Smith, H. A., Hallaham, C., & Lehrmen, S. N. (1988). Acyclovir suppression of frequently recurring genital herpes: Efficacy and diminishing need during successive years of treatment. *Journal of the American Medical Association, 260,* 2227-2230.

Summit, R. C. (1983). The child sexual abuse accommodation syndrome. *Child Abuse & Neglect, 7,* 177-192.

Suspect HIV infection in the sexually abused child. (1988, July). *Pediatric News,* pp. 2, 36.

Tanner, J. M. (1962). *Growth at adolescence.* Oxford: Blackwell Scientific Publications.

Thoennes, N., & Tjaden, P. (1990). The extent, nature and validity of sexual abuse allegations in custody/visitation disputes. *Child Abuse & Neglect, 14,* 151-163.

Thomas, J. N., & Rogers, C. M. (1981). Sexual abuse of children: Case finding and clinical assessment. *Nursing Clinics of North America, 16,* 179-189.

Thompson, S. (1988). Child sexual abuse redefined: Impact of modern culture on the sexual mores of the Yuit Eskimos. In S. M. Sgroi (Ed.), *Vulnerable populations* (Vol. 1, pp. 299-308). Lexington, MA: Lexington.

Tilelli, J. A., Turek, D., & Jaffe, A. C. (1980). Sexual abuse of children: Clinical findings and implications for management. *New England Journal of Medicine, 302,* 319-323.

Torrey, S. B., & Ludwig, S. (1987). The emergency physician in the courtroom: Serving as an expert witness in cases of child abuse. *Pediatric Emergency Care, 3,* 50-52.

Trepper, S., & Barrett, M. (1989). *Systemic treatment of incest.* New York: Brunner/Mazel.

Tunnessen, W. W. (1988). *Signs and symptoms in pediatrics* (2nd ed). Philadelphia: J. B. Lippincott.

U.S. Department of Health and Human Services. (1988). *National study on the incidence and prevalence of child abuse and neglect.* Washington, DC: Government Printing Office.

Van Leevwen, V. (1988). Resistances in the treatment of a molested 6-year-old girl. *International Review of Psychoanalysis, 15,* 149-156.

Watkins, S., & Quan, L. (1984). Vulvovaginitis caused by yersinia enterocolitics. *Pediatric Infectious Disease, 3,* 444-445.

White, S., Strom, G. A., & Santilli, G. (1987). *Guidelines for interviewing preschoolers with anatomically detailed dolls.* Unpublished manuscript, Case Western Reserve University, Cleveland, OH.

White, S., Strom, G. A., Santilli, G., & Halpin, B. M. (1986). Interviewing young sexual abuse victims with anatomically correct dolls. *Child Abuse & Neglect, 10,* 519-529.

White, S. T., Loda, F. A., Ingram, D. L., & Pearson, A. (1983). Sexually transmitted diseases in sexually abused children. *Pediatrics, 72,* 16-21.

Whitman, B. Y., & Munkel, W. (1991). Multiple personality disorder: A risk indicator, diagnostic marker and psychiatric outcome for severe child abuse. *Clinical Pediatrics, 30,* 422-428.

Williams, T. S., Callen, J. P., & Owen, L. G. (1986). Vulvar disorders in the prepubertal females. *Pediatric Annals, 15,* 588-605.

Woodling, B. A., & Heger, A. (1986). The use of the colposcope in the diagnosis of sexual abuse in the pediatric age group. *Child Abuse & Neglect, 10,* 111-114.

Woodling, B. A., & Kossoris, P. D. (1981). Sexual misuse: Rape, molestation, and incest. *Pediatric Clinics of North America, 28,* 481-499.

Index

AAP:
  Committee on Child Abuse &
    Neglect, 20, 100, 131-132
  Committee on Early Childhood,
    18, 100
Abrasions, 55, 57, 59
  superficial, 53
Abusive behavior, staged increase
    in contact, 8
Accidental trauma, 65-66
Accomodation syndrome, child
    sexual abuse, 10
Acid phosphatase, 78
Ally, during examination, 66
Ambiguous genitalia, 98
Anatomy:
  anal, 50
  female, 32
  male, 33-35
  See Genitalia
Anogenital:
  abnormalities, 95-97
  anogenital bleeding, 92
  anogenital irritation, 92
  appearance, 99
  bruising, 90, 92
  erythema, 84
  foreskin, 95

hair thread tourniquet syndrome,
    95
  labial agglutination, 95-96
  phimosis, 95-96
  urethral prolapse, 95-96
Anus, 66. *See also* Perianal
  anal penetration, 64-65
  anal sphincter, transection of,
    55
  anatomy, 50
  examination of, 73
  penile contact with, 57-58
  signs of abuse, 56-57
  tears, 55
  venous congestion, 55-56
Atopic dermatitis, 85

Bacterial vaginosis, 110
Balantis Xerotica obliterans, 87
Behavior:
  observations, documentation of,
    116
  parent's observations, 121
Bite marks, 55, 59
Bleeding:
  anogenital region, 92, 94
  infections, 92

pruritic dermatologic conditions, 92
STDs, 92, 100
vaginal discharge, 92-94
Blood, 78

Candida, 87, 112
Care giver interview, 23
Centers for Disease Control, 100, 101
Chancroid and Granuloma Inguinale, 111
Child welfare system, 134
Child's allegations, 122
Chlamydia:
    media, 103
    trachomatis, 103-104
Clitoris, 43
Clitoromegaly, 43
Clothing, lab findings, 80
Coercion:
    to be avoided, 66
    to maintain secrecy, 9
Colposcope, 67-69
Condyloma acuminata, 101, 106
Congenital abnormalities, 98-99
    ambiguous genitalia, 98
    distal vaginal agenesis, 98
    imperforate hymen, 98
    paraurethral cysts, 98
    phimosis, 98
    urethral diverticulum, 98
    vaginal septum, 98
Contusions, 53,
Court testimony, 131-133
Crohn's disease (inflammatory bowel disease), 84, 88
Custody battle, 122
    reliability of history in, 17

Damaged goods, 27
Definition of sexual abuse, 2
Delayed reporting, 17
Dermatologic disorders, 84
    dermatitis, 92
Developmental history, 121
Developmental issues, 21, 24-25
Diagnoses, documentation of, 119
Differential diagnosis, 82-99
Differential history, 83
Discharge, 73
Disclosure, 14, 60, 113-114
Distal vaginal agenesis, 98
Divorce, 122

Documentation, 18
    document of findings, 129
    examples of, 130-131
Documentation and conclusions: 128-135
    document findings, 129
    history, 128-129
    medical record, 128
    recording physical examination, 130-131
Dolls, use of, 25, 118
Drawings, use of, 25, 118
Dysuria, 54-55, 63, 100

Ectopic ureter, 95
Edema, 53, 55, 57
ELISA, 109
Emotional impact:
    abuse, 125
    assessment of, 118
    long-term effects of abuse, 125
Epididymus, 49
Erythema, 53
Erythromycin, 104, 105
Evaluation-criteria for emergent evaluation, 15-16
Examination:
    lighting, 68
    method of, 67-68
    oropharynx, 68
    photographs, 68
    physical abuse, 67
    privacy, 68
    Woods Lamp, 68
Excoriation, 84
Expert witness, 131, 133
External inhibitions, perpetrator, 7
Extragenital trauma, 52-53

Face of clock orientation, 33
Fact witness, 131
Family system, 123
    blended families, 123
    power structure within, 123
    in crisis, 127
Family members, 121
Feedback to family, 124
Fellatio, 59
Female anatomy, 42-47. *See* Genitalia
Fistula, 95
Fondling, 54-55, 63
Foreign objects, 55, 64, 65, 67, 94

Forensic:
  contents of rape kit, 76
  evaluation, 115
  evidence, 30, 77-78
Foreskin, 95
Formal records, documentation, 116
Fossa navicularis, 44, 58
Frog leg position, 69-73

Gardnerella vaginalis, 110-111
Genital findings:
  abrasions, 55, 57, 59
  anal tears, 55
  bite marks, 55, 59
  contusions, 53
  edema, 53, 55, 57
  extragenital trauma, 52-53
  fondling, 53
  foreign objects, 55, 64, 65, 67
  forensic evidence, 77-78
  in sexual abuse, 51-64
  labial adhesions, 61
  labial tears, 59
  lacerations, 54, 57, 62
  residual findings, 60
  scar tissue, 57, 61, 63
  seminal products, 57
  serythema, 53
  subtle findings, 62
  superficial abrasions, 53, 55-57
  superficial injuries, 60
Genitalia:
  clitoris, 43
  epididymus, 49
  female, normal, 42
  fossa navicularis, 44, 58
  hymen, 43-44, 54, 57, 60
  labia majora, 42
  labia minora, 42
  male anatomy, 49-50
  mons pubis, 42
  penis, 50
  posterior fourchette, 44, 58
  scrotum, 49
  testis, 49
  urethral meatus, 43
  vaginal vestibule, 43
Genital secretions, 58, 59
Genital warts, 100
Gonorrhea, 101-103
  penicillin allergic and, 103
  Thayer-Martin media, 102
  treatment of, 103
Group therapy, 126

Hair analysis, 78
Hair thread tourniquet syndrome, 95
Herpes:
  genitalis, 108
  HSV type I, 108
  HSV type II, 108
  infection, 108
  simplex, 101
  Tzank prep, 108
History, 10, 16, 128-129
  See Interview
  verbal evidence, 16
HIV, 101, 109-110
Huffman stages, 36, 60
Hymen, 43-48, 54, 57, 60
  change with positioning, 64-65
  fundamental orifice shapes, 44, 45-47
  hymenal membrane, 62, 63, 65
  hymenal orifice, 64, 72
  imperforate, 98
  size controversy, 64, 72-73

Inappropriate child sexual behaviors 120
Incidence:
  comparison of, 5
  of sexual abuse, 1-4
Infection, 86
  herpetic, 108
Injuries:
  accidental, 65-66
  impaling, 89
  local, 89
  straddle, 65, 89-90
  superficial, 60
  zipper, 90
Internal inhibitions of perpetrator, 7
Interview:
  child and, 23
  control during, 20
  diagnostic, 20
  essential elements of, 20
  family members, 121
  goal of, 20
  language issues and, 24
  modesty and, 25
  process of, 20-28
  questions during, 25-26
  the child, 115-116
  types of questions, 25-26
  validation, 116
  warm up, 22
Intragluteal coitus, 58

Kawasaki's syndrome, 84
Knee-chest position, 69, 71, 74
Kwell, 110

Labia:
    adhesions, 61
    agglutination, 95-96
    majora, 42
    tears, 59
Laboratory evaluation, 75-79
    specimens and collection of, 75-78
    standard studies, 76
Laboratory findings, 18, 30
    hair analysis, 78
Lacerations, 54, 57, 62
Lack of evidence (in physical exam), 30-31
Language during interview, 24
Lateral decubitus position, 69, 74-75
Legal:
    aspects of story, 117
    compliance with legal responsibilities, 28
    issues, evaluation of, 28
    services, 132-133, 134
Lichen sclerosus, 85-86, 90
Lighting during examination, 68
Local irritation, 85
Long-term effects of abuse, 10, 125
Longitudinal progression of sexual abuse, 8-9

Male anatomy, 49-50
    epididymus, 49
    penis, 50
    scrotum, 49
    See Genitalia
    testis, 49
Masturbation, 66, 120
Medical record, 128
Menstrual flow, 92
Mental Health Evaluation, 113-127
    components of, 115
    purpose of, 16
    methods of assessment of, 116
Metronidazole, 107, 111
Mongolian spots, 90
Mons pubis, 42
Motile sperm, detection of, 79
Motivation of perpetrator, 6, 7

Nonspecific complaints, physical and behavioral, 15

Oral-genital contact, 59
Oropharynx, examination of, 68

Paraurethral cysts, 98
Pediculosis pubis, 101, 110
Pedophilia, 6
Penicillin, 105
    when allergic to, 103, 105
Penis, 50
    inflammation of, 83
    penile penetration, 59-61
    penile stimulation, 58
    penile trauma, 59
Peri-urethral trauma, 54
Perianal:
    streptococcal cellulitis, 88
    venous congestion, 55
Perpetrator:
    characteristics of, 8
    dimensions of, 122
    personal history of abuse and, 122-123
Phases of abuse, 8-9
Phimosis, 95-96, 98
Physical:
    abuse, 6, 67
    evidence of sexual abuse, 17
    trauma by strangers, 68
Physical examination, 29-81, 66-75
    ally during examination, 66
    colposcope and, 67-69
    lack of physical findings and, 17
    photographs of, 68
    physical findings of, 82
    restraint during, 66
    tools of, 67
    vaginal speculum and, 67
    variables effecting likelihood of findings during, 51
Phytodermatitis, 91
Pinworm, 87-88
Positioning:
    during examination, 69-75
    frog leg, 33, 69-73
    knee-chest, 69, 71, 74
    lateral decubitus (cannonball position), 69, 74-75
Posterior fourchette, 44, 58
Post-traumatic stress disorder, 119-121
Power and control, 10
Preconditions for sexual abuse, 7
Prepubertal examination, 30
Prevalence, of sexual abuse, 2-4
    comparison of, 5

Privacy:
  during exam, 68
  during interview, 116
Prognosis of child, 125-126
Pruritus, 84
Psychological evaluation, 114
Psychotherapy, 126
  direct, 117
  indirect questioning, 117
  of witness, 133

Questioning:
  direct, 117
  indirect, 117
  of witness, 133

Rape, 52
Rape kit, 76-77
Recommendations for treatment, 124-125
Recording physical examination, 130-131
Rectal fissures, 55
Rectovaginal fistula, 95
Rectum, 79
Referrals, mental health, 114
Reporting sexual abuse, AAP guidelines for, 132
Residual findings, 55, 60
Resistance, overcoming, 7
Restraint, 66
Restrictive clothing, 94
Rugal symmetry, 57

Saliva specimen, 80
Sandbox vulvitis, 85
Scabies, 87
Scar tissue, 57, 61, 63
Scrotum, 49
Seborrhea, 85
Seminal:
  fluid, 78
  products, 57
Setting of interview, 22
Sexual contact, documentation of, 78
Sexual abuse:
  barriers to diagnosis of, 1
  categories of, 5
  complaints of, 14
  delayed reporting of, 17
  disclosure of, 134
  emotional impact of, 125
  evaluation of, 15

lack of physical findings of, 17
longitudinal progression of, 8
long-term effects of, 10
physical evidence of, 51
preconditions of, 7
reporting findings of, 132
signs of, 1, 14
suspicion of, 134
under reporting of, 1
Sexual abuse, anal findings:
  perianal venous congestion, 55
  rectal fissures, 55
  residual findings, 60
  rugal symmetry, 57
  transection of anal sphincter, 55
  traumatic findings, 63
Sexual abuse, diagnostic conditions confused with, 84-95
  anogenital bleeding, 92
  anogenital bruising, 90, 92
  anogenital erythema, 84
  anogenital irritation, 92
  atopic dermatitis, 85
  Balantis Xerotica obliterans, 87
  bleeding, anogenital region, 92, 94
  bleeding, infections, 92
  bleeding, pruritic dermatologic conditions, 92
  bleeding, STDs, 92, 100
  bleeding, vaginal discharge, 92-94
  candida, 87
  Crescentic hymenal orifice, 93
  Crohn's disease (inflammatory bowel disease), 84, 88
  dermatitis, 92
  dermatologic disorders, 84
  ectopic ureter, 95
  excoriation, 84
  fistula, 95
  foreign body, 94
  infections, 86
  Kawasaki's syndrome, 84
  Lichen sclerosis, 85-86, 90
  local irritation, 85
  menstrual flow, 92
  mongolian spots, 90
  perianal streptococcal cellulitis, 88
  photodermatitis, 91
  pinworm, 87-88
  pruritus, 84
  rectovaginal fistula, 95
  restrictive clothing, 94
  sandbox vulvitis, 85
  scabies, 87
  seborrhea, 85
  seborrhea lesions, 85

Shigella, 92
STDs, 86, 94
Stevens-Johnson syndrome, 84
streptococcus, 92
systemic infections, 94
vaginal discharge, nonbloody, 93-94
vaginitis, 86
varicella, 94
vascular nevi, 90-91
vulvar hemangioma, 93
vulvitis, 86
vulvovaginal problems, 84
vulvovaginitis, 95, 100
Yersinia, 92
zipper injury, 90
Sexual development:
    breast, 40-41
    Huffman stages, 36, 60
    male genitalia, 39, 42
    pubic hair, 36-40
    Tanner Stages, 36, 37-41
Sexually transmitted diseases (STDs),
    86, 94
    CDC recommendations for lab-
        oratory evaluation, 101
    cultures, 101
    incidence, 100
    See individual diseases, 100 -112
Shigella, 92
Social services, 132-135
    compliance with legal responsi-
        bilities in, 28
Sodomy, 56
Specimens:
    acid phosphatase, 78
    blood, 78
    collection of, 75-78
    forensic evidence, 77-78
    guidelines for, 77, 79-80
    hair analysis, 78
    seminal fluid, 78
    sperm, 78-79
Sperm, 78-79
Stevens-Johnson syndrome, 84
Straddle injury, 65, 90
Streptococcus, 92
Subtle findings, 62
Superficial:
    abrasions, 53
    injuries, 60
    trauma, 17
Syphilis, 104-105
Systemic infections, 94

T. pallidum, 104

Tanner Stages, 36-41. See Sexual
    development
Testes, 49
Tetracycline, 104, 105
Thayer-Martin media, 102
Trauma, superficial, 17
Traumatic findings, 63
Treatment:
    group therapy, 126
    of sexual abuse, 126-127
    psychotherapy, 126
Trichomoniasis, 101, 107
Trust of child, 2
Tzank prep, 108

Urethra:
    discharge, 101
    prolapse, 95-96
    meatus, 43
    urethral diverticulum, 98

Urethritis, 101

Vagina, 79
    vaginal discharge, 100-101
    vaginal septum, 98
    vaginal speculum, 67
    vaginal vestibule, 43, 72
Vaginal discharge, nonbloody, 93-94
Vaginitis, 83, 86
Validation:
    congruence, 117
    of child's story, 117
Varicella, 94
Vascular nevi, 90-91
Vulvar:
    coitus, 57, 63
    hemangioma, 93
Vulvitis, 83, 86
Vulvovaginitis, 83, 95, 100

Witness, 131, 133
    questioning of, 133
Woods Lamp, 68
Wrap-up session interview, 25

Yersinia, 92

Zidovudine, 109-110
Zipper injury, 90

About the Authors

Esther Deblinger, Ph.D., is the Clinical Director of the Center for Children's Support, Assistant Professor of Clinical Psychiatry, and Adjunct Assistant Professor of Pediatrics at the University of Medicine and Dentistry of New Jersey, School of Osteopathic Medicine. She was previously the Co-Director of the Child Sexual Abuse Diagnostic and Treatment Center at the Medical College of Pennsylvania and has extensive research, clinical, and teaching experience in the field of child sexual abuse. She received her B.A. from the State University of New York at Binghamton and her M.A. and Ph.D. in clinical psychology from the State University of New York at Stony Brook. She has been actively involved in the development of research examining the impact of child sexual abuse and the treatment of the resulting sequelae, and has published and presented research nationwide on these and other abuse-related issues. She is also the principal investigator for several studies, including an investigation of the psychosocial characteristics of nonoffending mothers, funded by the Foundation of UMDNJ, and a study of the efficacy of cognitive behavioral interventions for sexually abused children, funded by a grant from the National Center on Child Abuse and Neglect.

Martin A. Finkel, D.O., F.A.C.O.P., is an Associate Professor of Clinical Pediatrics, Medical Director, and Founder of the Center for Children's Support at the University of Medicine and Dentistry of New Jersey, School of Osteopathic Medicine. The center is a diagnostic resource for the forensic medical and mental health evaluation of sexually abused children for southern New Jersey. He was the first clinician to

149

introduce colposcopy on the East Coast for the evaluation of the sexually abused child, and he authored the first paper in the medical literature on the healing chronology of acute anogenital trauma as a result of sexual abuse. He has been a leader in the development of services for abused children in New Jersey, where he cochairs the Governor's Task Force on Child Abuse and Neglect and is a founding commissioner of the Children's Trust Fund. He is a strong advocate of multidisciplinary intervention strategies and has been instrumental in providing professional education for all disciplines throughout New Jersey. He is an Associate Editor for the medical section of *The Advisor*, a publication of the American Professional Society on the Abuse of Children, and he cochairs the Task Force on Medical Standards for the Evaluation of the Sexually Abused Child. His research interests continue to be directed at further elucidating the changes in anogenital anatomy as a result of trauma and interexaminer reliability in the interpretation of physical findings.

Angelo P. Giardino, M.D., M.S.Ed., is a Clinical Scholar at the Robert Wood Johnson Clinical Scholar's Program at the University of Pennsylvania School of Medicine, and a Research Fellow in the Division of General Pediatrics at the Children's Hospital of Philadelphia. He holds a master's degree in health professions education and has codeveloped a comprehensive resident curriculum on the evaluation of sexual abuse. Efforts are now under way to assess the impact of this curricular approach. In addition to his clinical responsibilities, Dr. Giardino is actively involved in several policy analysis projects that look at children's health care needs and their access to such care. He has served as a consultant to the U.S. Congress Office of Technology Assessment in this role. Currently, he is also a doctoral candidate at the Graduate School of Education at the University of Pennsylvania, where his work focuses on outcomes assessment in professional education. He discussed curricular approaches to sexual abuse evaluation at the Ambulatory Pediatric Association's spring 1991 meeting and at regional conferences in the Philadelphia area. He serves on the Pennsylvania Medical Society's Council on Education and Science, is a member-at-large of its Resident Physician's Section, and serves as a delegate to the American Medical Association's National Resident Physician's Section.

Eileen R. Giardino, Ph.D., R.N., M.S.N., is Assistant Professor of Nursing at La Salle University. She serves as Coordinator for the Adult Health and Illness Tract and teaches both undergraduate and graduate nursing students. She received her master's degree in nursing at Widener University and earned her Ph.D. in education at the University of Pennsylvania. Her research interests focus on caring in nurse-client interactions, symptom manifestation and management, and the symptomatology of adult survivors of physical and sexual abuse. In addition, she has developed programs in community-based health care directed at women's health care issues. She serves on the New Jersey State Nurses' Association District Board of Directors and is a member of its Peer Assistance Committee.

Julie Lippmann, Ph.D., a full-time faculty member of the Departments of Psychiatry and Pediatrics at the University of Medicine and Dentistry of New Jersey School of Osteopathic Medicine, has been the Clinical Child Psychologist at the Center for Children's Support at the university since its inception. After completing her bachelor's degree, magna cum laude in psychology, from Cornell in 1967, she earned an M.S.W. in clinical social work from Smith College School for Social Work in 1969 and received her doctorate in clinical psychology from Hahnemann University in 1986. She has worked as a clinician in a variety of medical and psychiatric setting with children, adolescents, and adults. Her postgraduate clinical work has centered almost exclusively on the evaluation and treatment of alleged child sexual abuse, at J. J. Peters Institute in Philadelphia and at the Center for Children's Support. She is a member of the Senior Research Team of Concerned Professionals for the Accurate Assessment of Child Sexual Abuse, a multidisciplinary task force of the New Jersey Psychological Association, and a collaborator in research and training endeavors associated with the university and the center. Currently, she is the principal investigator on a study on factors influencing the substantiation of sexual abuse in young children, funded by a UMDNJ Foundation grant, and is coinvestigator on an NCCAN-funded treatment outcome study.

Stephen Ludwig, M.D., F.A.A.P., is a Professor of Pediatrics at the University of Pennsylvania School of Medicine and Division Chief, General Pediatrics, at the Children's Hospital of Philadelphia. He has had a long-standing interest in the problems of abused children and their families beginning in the early 1970s, when he participated in one of the nation's first multidisciplinary child abuse teams at the Children's Hospital National Medical Center in Washington, DC. Since then, he has been the Child Abuse Consultant and Medical Director of the Child Abuse Program at the Children's Hospital of Philadelphia. He has also been the educational consultant for SCAN, Inc., an in-home treatment program for abused and neglected children. He has been active in research on various child abuse injuries, including the shaken baby syndrome, failure to thrive, and child sexual abuse. He has written many articles and chapters, particularly concerning the early identification of child abuse and emergency department management, and is senior author of *Child Abuse/Neglect: A Medical Reference*, with Dr. Alan Kornberg. He has served on the Executive Committee of the American Academy of Pediatrics Section on Child Abuse and Neglect and has been the Chairman of the Attorney General's Medical/Legal Advisory Board for the Commonwealth of Pennsylvania. He has lectured widely and has hosted a number of national conferences on the topic of the medical aspects of child abuse.

Toni Seidl, M.S.W., is a Social Work Supervisor at the Children's Hospital of Philadelphia. She coordinates psychosocial services for child abuse neglect, sexual abuse, and emergency services. She is a frequent writer, trainer, and consultant in the area of child abuse and child sexual abuse within the hospital and the larger community. She has received honors for her role as a child advocate and sits on the Board of the Support Center for Child Advocates. She is a member of the Pennsylvania Bar Association/Pennsylvania Medical Society's Task Force on Child Abuse and Neglect. In addition to her hospital-based clinical work, she is a member of the Field Cabinet of the University of Pennsylvania School of Social Work. She participates in research conducted by the child abuse team and is trained as a structural family therapist.